9 Things

You Simply

MUST DO

to SUCCEED in LOVE and LIFE

A PSYCHOLOGIST PROBES *the* MYSTERY *of* WHY
SOME LIVES REALLY WORK *and* OTHERS DON'T

—— ∞ ——

DR. HENRY CLOUD

THOMAS NELSON
Since 1798

NASHVILLE   DALLAS   MEXICO CITY   RIO DE JANEIRO

9 Things You Simply Must Do to Succeed in Love and Life

Published in Nashville, Tennessee, by Thomas Nelson. Thomas Nelson is a registered trademark of Thomas Nelson, Inc.

Thomas Nelson, Inc., titles may be purchased in bulk for educational, business, fund-raising, or sales promotional use. For information, please e-mail SpecialMarkets@ThomasNelson.com.

Published in association with Yates & Yates, LLP, Literary Agents, Orange, California.

Scripture quotations used in this book are from The New International Version, © 1973, 1978, 1984 by International Bible Society. Used by permission of Zondervan Bible Publishers.

Cover Design: Brand Navigation, LLC
            (The Office of Bill Chiaravalle) / www.brandnavigation.com
Interior: Inside Out Design & Typesetting

ISBN 978-1-59145-009-2
ISBN 978-0-7852-8916-6 (trade paper)

Printed in the United States of America
10 11 12 13 14 RRD 21 20 19 18 17

This book is dedicated to five "coaches"

who have selflessly guided me in

practicing the Nine Things.

I thank you for your guidance and commitment to me:

Dad, Toby, Peter, Greg, and Tony

CONTENTS

ACKNOWLEDGMENTS

Sealy Yates, my agent and friend, for helping "birth" this project, as opposed to several others that I did not want to do!

Byron Williamson, for your love of "message" and commitment to getting it out there in usable forms. This book is a result of that. And for your support and commitment to my overall "work," I thank you.

Joey Paul, for seeing the slant of these ideas and appreciating them enough to push the project through.

Jeana Ledbetter, for making sure the above three guys get along, and "greasing the wheels" of the process.

1

DÉJÀ VU PEOPLE

I DO NOT REMEMBER WHEN IT FIRST HAPPENED, but I do remember the feeling. It was like being in an episode of *The X-Files*. Or, more accurately, a strong *déjà vu*. I would be talking with someone, either in therapy or a consulting role, or even in a business situation, and I would think, *Wait a minute . . . I've met this person before.* I would try to remember where, and quickly I would realize that I could never have met that person in any other context. The feeling was an illusion. I would chalk it up to lack of sleep and move on.

But the experience kept repeating itself. And each time it had the same feel. It seemed like a moment in which time almost stopped. It always had that ring of *I know you from somewhere.*

As this sort of thing kept happening, I began to pay more attention to it. I had to know what was going on. I did not believe in people living past lives, but at certain times, certain people would seem so familiar that I was all but convinced that I knew them from somewhere—a different time and place. At least they reminded me of someone I had known before. But who could it be?

Then one day I noticed something. I was working on a business deal, and a particular situation came up. One of my friends in the deal said he would take care of the thing we were all discussing. He offered a way of handling it, and we moved on to the next issue. Everyone else at the table paid little attention, except to notice the fact that he had a good idea. But I had that same feeling again. *Why does this seem so familiar?* I asked myself. Then I realized that I did not know this man from somewhere else, nor did he remind me of anyone from my past. I had no familiarity with him other than what I had acquired during the time we had been friends and partners in this deal. What I felt had nothing to do with him as a person, or with anyone else for that matter. *It had to do with what he did.* It was the way he handled that situation. That was what I had seen before! It was what he *did* that seemed to stand out as familiar.

I had seen someone else do that same thing only a week before. I thought back to the previous situation. It was true: the man I was with at the moment and the person I had been with the week before, in similar circumstances and facing a similar dilemma, had responded in exactly the same way.

It was not who they were that gave me the sense of déjà vu. In fact, it was not really even the specifics of the actions they took and the solutions they proposed. Such details were unimportant to the larger principle I was observing. My feelings of déjà vu came from my growing sense that certain kinds of people, given certain circumstances, always face and resolve situations in the same way.

Then, I went on a little memory trip, and the mystery started to unravel a bit. The previous week was not the first time I had seen someone do what this business partner had done. I had seen other people in similar situations who had done exactly what my friend had done. And they had done it in a very similar manner. *It was as if all these people were the same person, in a way.*

But here is the interesting thing, and the thing that added to the confusion: all these people were very different from one another. They had different backgrounds, different personalities, different kinds of lives, different economic circumstances, and different abilities. But, they were the same in that they shared this particular way of handling life. And that commonality, I realized, was the déjà vu I kept experiencing. I was not encountering the same person over and over again; I was encountering a way of performing—a way of doing things that was so profound, and at the same time so simple and subtle, that it both stood out and was concealed at the same time.

REALIZATION NUMBER ONE

As I reflected upon the people who possessed this one pattern in common, something else became evident: *they were all successful in life.*

Now, admittedly, there are a lot of definitions of success, and I am not trying to tell you which definition you should adopt. What I am saying here is that all of these people in my déjà vu experience tended to accomplish success in love and life *in the ways that they defined success.* They moved forward. They did not stay stuck, repeating the same mistakes over and over again. They reached their goals and found what they were looking for in life. There must be a connection, I thought, with their success and this particular pattern of behavior that I kept observing.

I realized that I was not looking at a person; I was looking at a pattern. A way of behaving. Now that I recognized the pattern, I decided to look for it even more. A path that successful people took, given a certain set of choices.

This was realization number one for me:

> *The answer to "Who is this person?"*
> *was not a person at all. It was a way.*

REALIZATION NUMBER TWO

I thought I had pretty much solved the mystery. I just figured I had stumbled on some sort of personality type that superseded other clinical ways of categorizing people. I was recognizing a "successful" personality type. I could spot him or her by this way of behaving I had begun to identify.

Remember, though, "successful" in the way that I define it does not necessarily mean "successful" in the ways the world often defines it. It does not necessarily mean becoming wealthy, although some of the people in my déjà vu experiences were wealthy—even extremely so. Neither does it mean famous, though some of them were that as well. Nor does it mean monstrously accomplished and at the tops of their fields, although many were. I am not defining success by these symbolic measurements. I mean simply that these people were getting from life what they had decided they wanted. This could be in the realm of vocation, relationships, spiritual attainment, or otherwise. Life was working for them.

Then something else happened. I do not know why—maybe because I was no longer confused by the mystery. Whatever it was, I began to notice that, as I watched these people, I had the same sense of déjà vu but with a twist: there were other behaviors these people had in common in addition to the ones I had first witnessed.

I began to identify several "ways" of behaving and responding to situations that successful people had in common—ways that they handled themselves, their relationships, their work, and their lives.

Realization number two was that there was no identifiable personality type common to these successful people. Rather, it was this:

> *People who found what they were looking for in life seemed to do a certain set of things in common.*

There were *several* identifiable ways that these people "did life," and for the most part, they all practiced them.

REALIZATION NUMBER THREE

Now it was getting really interesting. I was becoming a researcher, student, sleuth, and voyeur all in one. Also, I was noticing some of these ways emerging in my own journey as a person as well. Over the years I had seen myself learn, change, and grow in many areas, though I still had some distance to go in others. Even though in no way did I have it all wired, the ways of doing life I saw working for others worked for me as well. They just seemed to be true.

Looking at these people and at my own life brought a further question: where did one learn these things?

Did these people have parents who operated in these patterns and modeled them for them?

Did they just internalize them from their families of origin (a proven psychological possibility), and really were no smarter or wiser than the rest of the pack?

Did they study wisdom material and discover these patterns as part of a diligent search for personal growth and success?

Did they get them from therapy?

Were they results of other growth steps they had taken and goals they had achieved (an interesting theoretical dilemma that we will touch upon later)?

Had mentors taught these ways to them as adults?

Had their spiritual development and enlightenment made the patterns available to them?

Did they learn them from reading books or attending seminars?

How did these people discover these principles? That was the operative question. What did they all have in common?

Surprisingly, I could not find any common source where all of these people downloaded the software on how to be so effective. They were from such diverse backgrounds that such a possibility was unthinkable. I would observe one man from a wonderful family who seemed to grow up doing the things I was looking at because his parents lived out those ways so clearly. Then I'd notice a woman who followed the same ways despite coming from a totally whacked-out family where her parents did not practice any of them.

There were others who had a history of not living out these patterns, then through therapy or some sort of growth path, adopted them along the way. And they performed them as effectively as those who had seemed to acquire them naturally. Others had to learn these patterns to survive emotionally, relationally, or vocationally. Then there were the "unconscious competent" types who had no idea what they were doing or why; they just did life this way and things went well for them.

After looking at these people over and over again, it was clear to me that they got these principles from different places—family, mentors, therapy, seeking, spiritual awakening, disaster, and so on. There was no consistent pattern for acquiring them that I could put my teeth into. But that said something even greater than if I had found a special history they all shared. Since there was nothing in common about these people's backgrounds and makeup, genes or histories, race, personality type, economic background, or IQ, these patterns of success do not reside in any one type of person. These patterns transcend all backgrounds, talents, and limitations.

Thus, *they exist on their own and are available to all of us.* They are not things that one person "possesses" and another does not, like a talent. Instead, we can all learn these patterns that work every time and lead to better lives. Here was my realization number three:

The truth is that no one is excluded. If you were not born with these patterns in place, you can learn them.

My belief is that once you do, life will never be the same.

My Déjà Vu Friends

Over the years I have encountered many people who gave me the déjà vu experience I described above. Even though I now realize that I never saw these people before, I often call them *my déjà vu friends* or *déjà vu people* because of having witnessed their successful "ways" over and over again. When I refer to *my déjà vu friend* or a *déjà vu person* in the following chapters, I am referring to those persons who practice those ways and enjoy the success that they bring.

I will introduce you to several of these déjà vu people and describe in detail the behaviors that made them successful. You will learn, as I did, why their successful ways of doing life often seem at first to be hidden. Meeting these people will flush their working principles into the open where you can see them in action and adopt them to achieve your own success in life and love.

2

NINE THINGS
HIDDEN IN PLAIN SIGHT

*Take care to get what you like,
or you will be forced to like what you get.*

—GEORGE BERNARD SHAW

I WENT INTO THE FIELD OF PSYCHOLOGY because I had a
strong desire to do something that involved helping others.
Psychology was a good fit for me. It combined a helping field
with interesting content areas, and I loved learning it all.

But my training did not teach me most of the things that we are
going to look at in this book. And that is one of the reasons I never
thought much about them, and also why so many other people who
are dedicated to personal growth miss them. Psychologists and
many others who want to improve life tend to look at (and rightly
so) the bigger developmental and existential issues that are crucial
to overcoming pain and getting out of distress. The truth is that
most of the times when we seek personal growth, it is because we
are hurting in some way. So we look at how to resolve the problems
of life such as depression, anxiety, and addictions from a perspective
of trying to get un-depressed, un-anxious, and un-addicted.

As a result, I was trained to focus on the growth of the person as an individual. I was trained to look at who the individual is in terms of how he is wired, or how he has been hurt, or how he is glued together in certain ways that are causing the distress. From there the focus is on how he can change as a person to feel better, relate better, and do better. The assumption is that if our life is not working well, we need to grow and change our equipment (our mind, personality, relational abilities, character, and so on). And that is true and profoundly helpful in many ways. We all need to grow and maintain our personal equipment. If we are depressed, then there are probably things inside that have gone wrong and need to be righted, particularly in the ways that we think, feel, process, behave, and relate to others. Therefore, most clinical training and most personal growth tends to focus on the person's progress in those abilities and the maturity of the "equipment" itself.

For example, we help people to overcome patterns of emotional detachment, passivity, negative thinking, perfectionism, narcissism, mistrust, control, and the like. Conquering all of these patterns, and others as well, has to do with making real changes in our makeup and how we are glued together as persons. And when people make these kinds of changes to their inner mechanisms, their lives really change. They feel better and relate better. Changing our equipment really works. As we become more whole, life improves. That is a fact.

All of these personal growth issues pull for our attention. They pull at us because there are great strides to be made when we focus on them. Much suffering ends, and we gain a lot of ground by working on becoming better, more mature people. But the focus of all those efforts tends to be on the health of the individual, sometimes to the exclusion of the *strategies* that a healthy person needs to learn to live in given situations.

That narrow focus was, in part, the reason I think I did not enlarge my own vision for such a long time. I was too busy focusing on the clinical perspective to the exclusion of the broader life perspective. But the truth is that even when a person becomes healthy, he can still fail to practice a lot of the ways that make life succeed. And conversely, people undergoing emotional problems can be practitioners of the ways of success.

I learned many of the ways of success from people who were depressed at the time, or working through trauma or anxiety. While they still had issues to resolve in terms of individual growth, they had attained the wisdom of what these patterns can do for us. Sometimes their simple drive for survival dictated the need for higher wisdom. I have often been amazed at how noble some people can be who are suffering significant emotional pain and distress. They inspire by their transcendent ways through which they succeed in life even while in pain. These people continued to pop up and cause me to say, *Wow! Who is that person?* You will meet several such people and see their ways in this book.

Their examples tell us that just because you do not have it all finished in terms of your personal growth does not mean that you cannot learn how to better handle life while you are getting there. I have seen that to be true zillions of times. Keep working on becoming healthy and whole. I am very committed to that process.

But, do not ignore the fact that, in addition, there are some ways of living life—having nothing to do with emotional health—that we all need to learn as well. In short:

Growth is not only about getting healthy
but about learning ways of living as well.

9 Things You Simply Must Do

THE INVISIBLE FORCE OF GRAVITY

Is gravity hidden? Well, it depends on whether you are flying or falling. Some people are very aware of the laws of gravity and use them to their advantage. They design things like airplanes, rocket ships, and satellites. They study gravity and other laws of physics and use them to accomplish great things. So to those who are flying, gravity is not hidden at all. To the contrary, it is embraced, loved, and obeyed.

But there are others who are not so aware. One who thinks a thirty-foot ladder leaning up against his house needs no side support is not really thinking of gravity very clearly. One who thinks that after several martinis he can still walk steadily has the same problem. It is not that they are opposed to the law of gravity; they are just not very mindful of it. Then, irrationally, they curse the ground when gravity does what gravity does and they fall.

Is the law of gravity hidden to these people, unable to be discovered? Not at all. Neither are the "ways" of doing life hidden from those who fail to practice them. They could have learned them somewhere, and might even have heard of them at times. But instead they broke themselves on the laws by not paying attention to how they work in day-to-day reality. Gravity is just reality. It is. Obey it and it will help you do great things. Even fly. Ignore it and you will fall and hurt yourself.

In observing people who possess the qualities I have been speaking of, I have discovered nine principles that are like gravity. These Nine Things are there, and we can work with them to achieve great results in success, relationships, love, and other areas of life. Or we can ignore them and suffer the consequences. Now, I would not say that my particular way of communicating these Nine Things is as certain as the proven laws of physics. But what I would say with confidence is this: working with a lot of people and practicing these Nine Things myself has shown them to be utterly dependable. I am convinced that you can count on them to help you avoid hitting the pavement.

Where there are exceptions I believe that other mitigating factors are at work, and the Nine Things are still true. For example, when the wind blows, and a piece of paper does not fall directly to the ground, it does not mean that gravity is not working. It means that other forces in that situation are also at play. But day to day, drop your paper and it is headed for the ground. You can place your bets. The Nine Things are like that. You can bet on them. In those exceptional cases when they do not seem to be working, other forces are at play and greater wisdom is needed for that day.

So, my goal here is to help you to look at these Nine Things as do the people who practice them. They would not ignore any of these principles without good reason. That is how strongly they hold to them. Sometimes they would suspend them or not execute them, just like one seems to do with gravity when he or she goes skydiving or scuba diving. On any other day, a wise person would not ignore gravity by jumping out of a plane or off the deck of a boat in deep water. But at particular times people do so for other reasons besides denial. They have a purpose in seeming to ignore gravity, and they put precautions in place that make them less vulnerable to the laws of "going down." They carry a parachute or a tank of air. The laws governing falling and the dangers of the deep are still operative, but in those situations people suspend the usual practice of obeying them for a good reason. There is a higher goal involved, and they carry the equipment necessary to deal with the potential downside.

For example, indulge me while I jump ahead a little. Take Principle Two of the Nine Things: the law regarding putting an end to negative things. Don't forbearance, perseverance, and long-suffering dictate that one keeps working with bad situations, thus "disobeying" the law that says to get rid of negatives? Of course. But the difference between people who do that with the law in view and those who do not is huge. The person who is not mindful of the principle will continually be abused in one negative situation after another. But the mindful one *intentionally* works with the bad situation *purposefully* to turn it around, and makes sure to carry a parachute or a tank of air in the process. These wise ones are still obeying the reality of the principle. They respect the laws so much that when they "break" them, they understand what they are doing and break them for good reason and with proper safeguards. They break them mindfully, not ignorantly.

So, like gravity, these principles are not hidden. Some people find them and they benefit from them. But there are many reasons why we often do not see things until a certain time. That is okay, and certainly a part of growth itself.

In fact, you might have had certain forces at work against you that kept you unaware of these principles. See if you recognize any of these forces:

- A background or history of close association and identification with people who were not finding success in love or life

- Emotional or relational pain that kept you in survival mode so much that learning mode seemed a luxury

14

- Religious teaching that focused so much on guilt, shame, and "good and bad" that there was not enough room to learn wisdom and love

- Relationships that have been so hurtful and did not work so many times that you gave up hope on finding one that would

- Hitting a ceiling on reaching goals, or failing to realize your goals and potential so much that you came to think that success was just for others

- Believing that things are possible if you just "try harder" or "get more committed," leading to repeated instances of trying again but expecting different results

- Seeing that following the "ways" called for change, and change is sometimes frightening

These negative forces all have the common strain of being taught by experience that it just won't work. Or, *success is not out there for me anywhere.* As a result, many people do just what the parable of the talents describes. They bury their abilities, potential, and resources because of fear (Matthew 25:14–30). They have decided that it is just not worth it to hope or try because nothing is going to work. They cannot see a way out of their situation. And they have often blamed themselves and often stopped looking.

But the message of this book is that there is nothing special about the people who do make it work. Success is not about them—their unique talents or skills. It is about the principles of life and wisdom that transcend any of our own abilities or lack thereof. And if you do not allow failure, past experience, or naiveté to blind you to learning how successful people do it, you can do it too.

I believe in the reality of wisdom. I believe that, like Solomon said, the commands of wisdom "will prolong your life many years and bring you prosperity" (Proverbs 3:2). Solomon further says that the entire earth was created by wisdom: "By wisdom the LORD laid the earth's foundations, by understanding he set the heavens in place" (Proverbs 3:19). In other words, the earth and how it works is not random. There is an order to the ways that things work. Life was created with laws that govern how it works. There are laws that govern success just as gravity governs falling. If we can learn to follow these laws, we can live better lives.

That is what I believe about the Nine Things: *they are wisdom.* In the upcoming chapters, we will see where they come from, how they work, how to put them into practice, and the pitfalls of not following them.

Are the Nine Things the "ultimate wisdom" pieces of life? I do not think so. First of all, I would never claim to understand the "ultimate" anything. But more than that, I think there are other principles even more foundational than the ones we will look at here. For example, love, truth, and faith are not in the list of Nine. Those are about as ultimate and foundational as you can get. We cannot talk about all of the wisdom in the universe in one book. If you wrote merely a few paragraphs on each of the verses written by Solomon, the wisest man ever, the result would be a volume too stupendous to comprehend in any manageable chunk of time.

Besides, I do not like "ultimate" anythings, because there is always another "more ultimate" to follow. That is not how I look at the Nine Things. There are many more life principles than these, so obviously they cannot be the ultimate or the end-all to anything.

I chose them for three specific reasons.

First, they are paths or patterns of behavior that really do make a huge difference in the lives of those who practice them. I consider them uncontainable in their fruitfulness.

Second, avoiding these principles can lead to disastrous consequences, such as the loss of love, dreams, goals, potential, relationships, and trust—even faith itself.

Third, these principles are often ignored. I seldom hear them talked about as specific patterns to be observed and diligently applied.

For those reasons, I have chosen to write about these Nine Things. They are not ultimate, nor are they exhaustive of all you need to know to succeed in life. But they are enormously profitable if practiced, detrimentally consequential if ignored, and often overlooked. And they can be learned and mastered, just as you can learn and master the laws of nature to soar above the clouds at 30,000 feet.

As Solomon says again about wisdom, "Hold on to instruction, do not let it go; guard it well, for it is your life" (Proverbs 4:13). So in this book we will look at the lives and experience of my déjà vu friends and others to see how they can instruct us, as well as at the gifts of wisdom that God provides in so many ways. The wisdom we glean through such instruction will help us to find more and more of the life we were created to live. These principles need no longer remain hidden. You can put them to work for you as do so many others who are no better, no more gifted, or no smarter than you. They simply see gravity, respect it, and let it take them to a higher view.

Let's jump in now and look at the nine life principles to learn how they can help you, too.

3

PRINCIPLE 1:
DIG IT UP

*Choice of attention—to pay attention to this and ignore that—is to the
inner life what choice of action is to the outer. In both cases, a man is
responsible for his choice and must accept the consequences,
whatever they may be.*

—W. H. AUDEN

W E ARE HERE TODAY IN AN EXTRAORDINARY BUILDING," I
said to the audience. "Look at the design, the way it all
works. Look at those huge beams that hold it all together, and how they magically stretch all the way across the
expanse of the ceiling. Look at how high the walls are, and yet they
just seem to stand there. Notice how warm it is in here though you
know it is cold outside. The design of this place meets both our
appreciation of beauty and our need for protection from the
weather. And we all feel safe. Not one of us is worried that it is
going to fall down in the middle of the seminar."

We all took a moment to revel in the structure we had been
somewhat ignoring all day. It truly was something to behold.

"Now, I have a question for you. Does anyone know where this arena came from?" I asked. "Anyone know where it originated?"

No one said anything. So, I tried again. "Anyone want to tell me where this building originated from?"

"A builder built it," someone offered.

"True," I said, "but from where did it *originate?* Let me tell you a great mystery. We are standing here in a physical world, the real world that we can see and feel, taste and touch. In the case of this building, we can use it, stand in it, reach out and touch it. It is the real thing, as we say. But, where did this building in the real, physical, *visible* world come from?

"It came from the *invisible* world of a toddler's soul," I told my audience. "I guarantee you, that is where this awesome coliseum came from. This visible arena came from the invisible soul of probably a twenty-month-old child.

"One day, years ago, a little girl, having just learned to walk, was exploring her world more and more. She was in the den one evening right before bedtime, getting in the last few minutes of play. Then, something happened.

"She took a few blocks, and instead of her normal pounding them down and throwing them about, she stacked one on top of another. And . . . they stayed! Then, she took another block, placed it on top of the second one, and it stayed there too! As she stacked the fourth block, something leapt inside her. She felt excitement and glee; she laughed and exclaimed, 'Yaaay!' She was so excited to see that a tower of blocks could be built and stay there, one upon the other.

"Right at that moment, Mommy and Daddy noticed too. Their excitement matched hers as they clapped and said 'Yaaay!' along with her. 'That's so good, Susie!' they exclaimed. Everyone was enjoying the moment, but what was really happening was much more than just a moment's joy. It was a miracle. For Susie was discovering two of the most powerful forces in the universe: talent and desire. She found that when she worked with blocks, something inside of her felt alive and filled her with joy, and she desired to do it more. She added another block, and when it fell, she did not quit. She built her tower over and over again, laughing and exclaiming with each iteration of her creation. Her parents shared in her delight. Her talent for interacting with spatial design had just had its first day in the outside world.

"Not too long after that, in her preschool and kindergarten, she loved the hours spent drawing and painting in art class. When she took the pencil or brush in her hand, something special happened. Not only did it provide a different level of enjoyment than soccer, but her teachers noticed it as well. They encouraged her with every drawing.

"Then she also found the same sort of attraction to her math classes—an attraction lacking in literature and English. Although she was good at most of her studies, math and art seemed really to give her that 'alive' feeling inside, as opposed to just doing the chore of her assignment or homework. In fact, sometimes in English class she would find herself hiding a paper beneath her textbook on which she would draw the medieval castle described in the story.

"At the same time, her parents encouraged her in her studies and praised her when she did well. When she struggled, they took the time to help her and held her feet to the fire when she wanted to blow off her work. They enforced their 'homework first and play later' rule. The discipline they provided was becoming a part of her, for when she went to college and was away from them, she studied while others partied. As a result she graduated with honors in her major, went to graduate school, and became what she had dreamed of becoming since high school: an architect.

"After being diligent and creative in her early jobs doing basic drafting and small buildings, she was given more and more responsibility. She remained faithful with her talent and had the character to bring it to fruition. One day she was promoted to partner at her firm, which meant a chance to do the big jobs. Her promotion came just as the city was planning a new event center, and they were asking for proposal drawings.

"Many more steps were involved, but in the end it was Susie's design that won the bid, and it was her design that created the arena that we are in today. And here is the point: this reality, this physical reality of a real structure in the real visible world, came from the invisible reality of a little girl's talent. It came from her soul."

The invisible world is always where the visible originates.

I continued.

"Everything that you can see around you, began in the invisible world of someone's soul. It was first a talent, then a dream. It came into being because of talent, discipline, and desire, all invisible ingredients which live in the souls of men and women. A building, a business, a good marriage, a healthy family, a social movement of change, new technology, a medical breakthrough, a beautiful wedding celebration, a realization of a new hobby and skill, and all of the other things and activities that we see around us in this physical world, all begin in the souls of human beings. That is the order of the original creation itself. The visible creation came from the invisible God. He dreamed it, saw it, spoke it, and it was. And he has passed on to us that same way of creating. He has put talents, desires, abilities, dreams, values, and zillions of wonderful things into the souls of humans so that we can bring about beautiful things in life. And they always start from the inside and work their way to the outside world."

But . . .

Then I told my audience about another building that was just as beautiful as the one we were in that day. It was just as big, just as amazing in its design, the acoustics were just as awesome, and it held just as many people as the one we were using. The capacity of this other building would fully meet the urgent needs of the community. There was just one problem: it didn't exist in the real world, in the visible, physical world where an audience can actually sit in real chairs and listen to a real performance. We wouldn't be able to find this building anywhere, not in this town or anywhere else. Why? The sad reality is that this auditorium was never built. It is still stuck in the invisible world of another child, one we will call Jenny.

Jenny's initial experience was similar to Susie's. When she was a toddler, she sat on the floor of the den one day and made a similar tower. She felt the same excitement, the same quickening of her spirit inside when she saw the blocks stand one upon the other. She was so excited! Like Susie, Jenny felt alive.

But, when Jenny's father walked in, his reaction was quite different from that of Susie's parents. He scolded her for making a mess in the middle of the floor. He destroyed her stack with a harsh sweep of his foot and told her to put the blocks away. She cried, and he told his wife to take her to bed. He said it was too late for her to be up anyway, and he was tired of listening to all the noise she made.

Later, when Jenny was drawn to art and following the path that Susie took, her father told her that she would never get a job with her silly drawings and to get to work on something practical. He rarely even asked about her schoolwork, and certainly didn't build into her life the discipline that Susie was learning, the kind she would need to sustain her no matter what she studied. He was harsh in other ways as well, and slowly Jenny drifted away from studies altogether. She just hung out with her boyfriend, who was not into school. At times she would still doodle on pads of paper, passing the time, but then she would toss them into the trash.

Jenny went to college but she didn't really feel like studying, since she didn't know what she wanted to do. Mostly she just wanted to be with her boyfriend and other friends, and she partied with them much of the time. She managed to pass her classes, but without any clear direction she just picked a major at random and plodded along until she finished. After graduation she went to work in the human resources department of a large company—a far cry from architectural design. Mostly, the only thing she looked forward to was the weekends, not designing a building. But as we know from Susie's experience, there was a beautiful building still inside Jenny's soul, waiting to come out. Would it ever see the light of day?

YOUR HEART'S DESIRE

Remember the déjà vu person in chapter one, the one I seemed to keep meeting over and over who put into practice the "ways" that successful people live? If he were an architect, you can bet that he was building buildings because he was living out the desires and dreams of his soul. Was he Susie or Jenny?

The truth is, *he could be either,* and is probably a combination of both. If you recall, we noticed that déjà vu people come from a lot of different backgrounds. They might come from healthy families, where the parents were like Susie's, encouraging them to follow what was deep in their hearts and was true to them. They might also come from backgrounds like Jenny's—with dysfunctional families where one learns very little about the principles that help a person find success or develop their talents.

One thing is for sure: if a déjà vu person was a Jenny, he made a change somewhere along the line. He did the first of the Nine Things. He learned that life comes from the inside.

What lies deep inside is where the real life is. And this déjà vu person spent some time listening to it, looking for it, digging it up, and putting it into practice. He found what lay deep in his heart, below the surface, and invested it in life.

To make a successful life, the déjà vu person:

- Becomes aware of his dreams, desires, talents, and other treasures of his soul

- Listens to them and values them as life itself

- Takes steps to develop them, beginning in very small ways

- Seeks coaching and help to make them grow

- Does not care as much about his results as his essence, but just continues to express them wherever he can

Principle One can be expanded this way: the reality of the life we see and live on the outside is one that emerges from the inside, from our hearts, minds, and souls. It is our internal life that creates our external one. So, to find our lives we must find what lies below the surface of our skin. We must look at, listen to, discover, and be mindful of our internal life—of such things as our talents, feelings, desires, and dreams.

Buried Treasure

So why don't we all seek this internal life? Well, Jenny can tell us of one reason. We have all had experiences that make our internal life unavailable to us. Those experiences can come from family, teachers, friends, church, teachings, jobs, failure, some subculture you live in, traumatic incidents, lack of resources or opportunities, and hundreds of other sources. As a result, we find ourselves living lives that are out of touch with the very center of life itself: with our hearts, minds, and souls. As Jenny can tell us, it is possible just to float through school, or even through the beginning of one's career, completely out of touch with who you are and what you want.

But it is not only in the arena of work or career that this disconnection can happen. It happens in many other areas as well, such as in significant relationships. There are people who merely float along in their relationships as blindly as Jenny floated along her career path, out of touch with the feelings and drives of their heart. It is the passion that lies below the surface that makes relationships alive and keeps them growing. Being out of touch with that inner passion can cause a relationship to go stale or even to fail.

Robert and Melissa found this to be true. He was a "nice" guy, always trying to please her as best he could. Competent, successful, and loving, on the surface he looked like the model husband. But beneath the surface, things were not as good as they appeared.

When this couple came to me, he was suffering from a total loss of sex drive. And she no longer felt attracted to him; she did not find him exciting any more.

As I worked with Robert and Melissa, I found that a kind of settled routine had taken over their relationship. Mostly from his side, there had been a "loss of the soul." In his dutiful pleasing of her, and also in his fear of upsetting her (she had a bit of a quick temper), he had slowly put to sleep any of his own desires that conflicted with hers. He ignored them, and he also ignored the resulting feelings of resentment that were the residual effects of some of his niceness. He had gone dead inside, but he continued to function in all areas that were visible on the surface. It was the *invisible* that had been ignored. But as we saw with Susie and Jenny, it is the invisible that gives rise to the visible. So as a result of ignoring the invisible, Robert and Melissa were starting to see their relationship suffer.

When we began to "dig it up," we got to Robert's heart again. First, it involved his being honest about some things that he did not like, although he had acted as if those things were not really problems. Slowly, as he became more honest, he actually expressed some of the things that troubled him within the relationship. Then he got to the big issue: he expressed the things that he actually wanted the two of them to do but was afraid to push her to do—*his desires*. These desires could be small or large, his preference for dinner or how to spend their vacation. It did not matter, for all of it was his heart. Slowly he began to express these desires, and as a result the couple got into conflict.

Then, with sparks flying as we worked with their ability to resolve the conflict, something else happened. Robert found his libido, and Melissa found him much more enticing. Passion had returned. Why? Sexual technique training? Not at all. Romance coaching? No need for that either. Just the chemistry of two fully alive individuals in an honest relationship where they learned to express and respect each others' desires, and then be active enough to put them into action, like when they first met. They were "building a building." And the building was a thriving marriage that had seemed dead. Their marriage was becoming visible in the outside world for them to see and enjoy. They could thrive in it and be protected from the stormy weather of life, realizing the full benefits of its design. But these benefits came from digging up the inside and investing it back into life, facing the invisible and making it visible.

But to dig this deeply means that we must face some fears and obstacles. What about the list above? What can you identify in your own life that has caused you to bury your treasure? Was it a harsh parent like Jenny's? A tough relationship? A lack of opportunity or resources that caused you to give up? A subculture that put you down? Other people who did not like what you brought forth from inside your heart and soul? The times you tried and failed?

One thing is sure:

> *There is no shortage of things in life*
> *that can cause you to bury your heart and soul.*

The truth is, however, that those who succeed in any aspect of life have not allowed those influences to keep their dreams and desires hidden. They have dug them up, faced their fears, taken risks, failed, gotten up again, and found that they could indeed build a beautiful building.

Julia was such a person. When she was in her early twenties, she fell in love and married Devin, a "winner"—the type of person who knew who he was and where he was going. Devin pursued his career, built a big electronics business, and achieved considerable success. Although Julia had always enjoyed school and directing various service projects, after marriage she quit doing much with her or-ganizational talents. Overshadowed by his drive and aggressiveness, she became more a follower of his life and career.

At first the cause of her withdrawal from the things she enjoyed seemed to be the demands of her role as mother of young children. But there were other causes more subtle. Devin put her down. He had an ability to make her feel inferior and stupid when it came to things in the realm of work. He had many ways of dominating, but the most harmful were those in which he discounted her abilities. Slowly she retreated into the area where she did not have to compete with him: that of being a mother. She performed very well in that role and just put her other talents aside.

As many such stories go, years later Devin became bored with the woman he had subdued and fell in love with someone from work. He left Julia behind. After the divorce, she did not know what she was going to do. She felt lost.

Her friends would have none of that, however. Some of them knew her before she married Devin and knew of her outstanding talents and abilities. They pushed her to step out. She resisted, feeling that she was "stupid" and could not really make the kinds of decisions required to do the kinds of work they were telling her to go for. But her friends would not hear of it, so Julia relented and one of them hired her to work in her company.

Julia was not long in her new job before she began to put her hand to organizing things around her, even beyond her assigned duties. Then she discovered that to help the company as much as she wanted, she needed to acquire some computer skills that she did not possess. The thought both frightened and excited her. She wanted to do it, but she could hear *You won't be able to learn that!* reverberating in her head. But on the sly without others knowing it, she took a class at a community college and learned the necessary programs. Gradually, she offered to help on some of the bigger projects at work. Soon employees from other departments turned to her for help. She was gaining a reputation. Not long after, she was moved to a new position in more complicated operations, and within a year she was running a division with big budgets.

As she related her story, she said one thing that was quite telling: "I had somehow lost touch with what I liked to do, and slowly I had come to believe that I couldn't do it. It was like a part of me had died. Then, when I thought about doing it again, I was too afraid to try. If it weren't for Molly making me step out and try that little job, I don't know where I would be today."

Notice the progression.

1. She lost touch with her "likes"—talents, desires, and so on.

2. She allowed them to become buried.

3. She considered doing them again, but was afraid.

4. She was tempted to back away and keep them buried.

5. She got a push to step out and ventured a little step forward.

6. The investment of the little step multiplied over time to a full visible reality.

7. Julia was alive again.

This choice, I believe, is always put before each of us, every day. We are given a heart full of treasure and talent, feelings and desires. In short, *potential realities.* God has granted to us a heart, mind, and soul full of potential realities for whatever our situation might be, perhaps one of the following:

- A relationship (like Robert's)

- A career (like Julia's)

- Being part of a neighborhood or community, or wherever we find ourselves

- A fulfilling hobby or skill (other than vocation)

- Service and volunteering for a good cause

- Church and spiritual pursuits

- Creative pursuits

It is our job to *dig up* whatever potential we have in whatever situation we are in, and then to invest it and see it grow. The choice is whether we are going to allow fear and experiences to keep our potential buried, or choose to step out in faith and see that potential turn into reality.

One of the best examples of this is found in the parable of the talents, a favorite story of mine. In this parable in Matthew 25:14–30, the master entrusts three servants with various amounts of money to be invested while he is away. He returns at a later date and checks out what they have done. Two of the servants stepped out, took risks, were diligent, and earned a handsome profit for the master. The third was afraid and buried his treasure in the ground. He returned only what he was originally given.

The first two are rewarded, and the last one is scolded and loses the little that he had. Is that a picture of reality or what? Those who take what they possess, invest it in life, and are diligent and faithful with it over time, grow and build something good. But those who allow fear to keep them from stepping out, *not only fail to increase what they have, they actually lose it.*

That is what seems to happen over and over when people bury their internal, invisible treasure—their dreams, talents, and passions. When it is buried and protected, it does not remain vibrant and alive. Just as Robert, Melissa and Julia discovered, the good potential ceases to thrive and begins to die when it remains unused. It is in a very real sense, lost, just as the parable predicts it will be.

Not so with the déjà vu person who lives out this particular "way." He does not allow the treasures of his heart, mind, and soul to remain below the surface. He digs them up, puts them into practice, invests them, and gets a return. Even when it means, as Julia or Robert found, that risk, learning, pain, conflict, and other hard things are involved. It does not matter, and it does not stop him.

---

*Those who succeed in life cannot ignore
their hearts, minds, and souls.*

Déjà vu people listen to what is going on inside, good or bad. They bring it up and deal with it. If it is good, they find a proper place for its expression and growth. If it is not so good, they deal with that as well, as we shall see. But either way, the invisible things that lie within are recognized as the source of life, and they are not ignored.

As Solomon said about minding what is inside the heart: "Above all else, guard your heart, for it is the wellspring of life" (Proverbs 4:23).

Above all else is pretty strong language, don't you think? We can see why Solomon uses those words when we realize that without guarding what is inside the heart, no building would ever be built, no family ever restored, no career ever reborn, no volunteer movement ever realized.

His phrase, *wellspring of life,* says it all. It means the place from which it all comes. Success and failure alike arise from what is going on inside, and the wise person is one who pays attention.

Not All that Is Buried Is Treasure

In the examples of Susie and Julia, we see things buried in the heart that are good. Dig them up and you find an architect and a competent organizer. Those are great finds. But not all that lies below the surface is so wonderful.

In Robert's case, while he dug up his passion and desire, he had to wade through a few pools of resentment, anger, and conflict as well. Julia also had some demons in her heart. She had to face the fear that was below the surface—the hurt that her husband had inflicted, the shame of allowing herself to be treated poorly, and the loss of so many things related to her marriage.

If we dug into Jenny's heart, we would find much that is not at all pretty. We would find hurt and anger at her father, feelings of being used by the boyfriends she gave herself to in her attempts to find male acceptance, fears of inadequacy at her lack of confidence and discipline, and shame for the lost years. Many of those things would not be her fault, so to speak, but all of them would reside in her soul and would be her responsibility.

But, if Jenny would dig these ugly things up, face them, and deal with them appropriately, she would find that by going through the "death" experience of facing the negative things inside, a resurrection would occur. The good things that had died would come back to life. That was the experience of Robert and Julia, and it could be yours as well.

It is the path of my successful déjà vu friends, for sure. They don't look inside just to find winning lottery tickets. They look inside to find whatever is there. They "guard their hearts with diligence," as the proverb says in another translation. They oversee it, and deal not only with the good feelings and dreams but the problems as well.

The wisdom of their approach is this: they know that by dealing with the bad stuff inside, two things will happen.

First, they rid themselves of the pain or sickness they are carrying around and the effects it is having or could have in their life. They know that if they leave it untouched, it will only become a cancer that gets larger.

Grief that is ignored turns into depression or hopelessness. Hurt turns into cynicism, lack of trust, or worse. Anger turns into bitterness and hatred. The list goes on, but déjà vu people know that just as you do not want a tumor growing in your brain, you do not want one growing in your heart either. There are no benign tumors of the heart. They all spread their cancer into the visible world, where they destroy all that one is trying to build—relationships, reaching goals, happiness, and fulfillment. No matter what a person is trying to accomplish, if he is walking around with unresolved matters of the heart, his goals will be negatively affected.

And secondly, the wise déjà vu person knows that *every time he faces one of those sicknesses in the heart, something better and larger emerges.* Either new solutions are found in facing and solving problems, or new aspects of the soul are discovered. When we face our demons and our pain, we "reclaim the land" of our hearts and souls. You come through that suffering being better than who you were when you went in. You get back what had been taken and find extra character to boot. These wise people understand all that, and they enter into the process willingly.

What you dig out of your heart will be a mixture of both good and bad. Dreams, talents, pains, and also ugly stuff like resentment or hatred will all reside there. Both the good stuff and the bad can be scary. The dreams can call you to get out of your slumber and take a risk. The ugly stuff can shatter your nice picture of yourself. But both are you, and that is okay. It means that you are human, and God loves all of you regardless of the good or the bad, the divine or the ugly.

Your job is to dig it all up and then do one of two things: sow it, or throw it away.

If it is good, like a talent, a dream, a desire, or something else that you want to see grow, sow it. Plant it. Water it. Fertilize it. That is what Julia did, and her outside life grew. That is what Susie did, and we found ourselves in a beautiful building. There is no telling what we will find in the future as a result of what you sow now. If what you dig up is painful or ugly, throw it away. That means to process it, mourn it, heal it, grieve it, repent of it, or whatever it takes to work it out of your system. You are growing a garden in your heart; some things you wish to increase, and others you need to weed out. Either way requires caretaking. That is your job as guardian of your heart.

Take Appropriate Risks

Julia and Robert did not just dig things up and let them lie there. They took the risks of investing their invisible treasures in the visible world. Julia stepped out and tried her skills. She tried a job in spite of her fear of failing at it. She took a class even when the voice inside her head told her she could not learn. She spoke out in meetings with bosses when she had an idea. With each new victory, she gained more ground in the external world as the interior world of her heart and soul were expanding.

Robert did likewise. When he discovered what he felt and what he wanted, he took the risk of being honest with me and with his wife. He took the risk of not backing down in the conflict as he had done for years. He took the risk of making his desires known, and then he took the big risk of pursuing them in the relationship.

There is very little growth and reward in life without taking risks. As the parable says, the one who buried his treasure in the ground did so to avoid risk of loss, failure, and disapproval. In the end, though, he reaped all three of these disasters. Clearly . . .

Avoidance of risk is the greatest risk of all.

Taking risks, however, does not mean that when you discover a treasure in your heart you should just roll the dice. That is not what any of these people did. Julia was diligent and followed her path with wisdom and calculation. She took it one step at a time. She did not say, "Since I have this organizational talent, I think I will pull up and start a new business," then invest her life savings and divorce settlement into some lame-brained idea. That is not what it means to take risks in a wise sense.

As Solomon tells us, "The wisdom of the prudent is to give thought to their ways, but the folly of fools is deception" (Proverbs 14:8). Julia did not deceive herself into thinking that her nascent talent was an ability. She took one small step at a time, giving much thought and prudence to each. But each step built on the other, and each was risky in its own right. That is far different than betting the farm in an impulsive way.

The same was true of Robert. He took risks with Melissa, but they were in the contexts of wisdom and "giving thought to his ways." He did not just "find himself," as the popular culture says, and realize that she was not making him happy, and then jettison the spouse that was holding him back from his fulfillment. That is not growth at all. In fact, that is a resistance to growth.

Growth is when you take the new things that you dig up and discover, and then integrate them with the rest of who you already are—things such as your values, relationships, and loves. Robert took his newly discovered feelings and truths and integrated them with his values of commitment to a marriage, his love for Melissa, and all the things he believed in. That is true growth and integration.

A successful déjà vu person is not afraid of the downside of taking risks. But he does not jump off cliffs and then expect good things to happen. That is what the devil tempted Jesus to do—to give up all reason and rational thinking, jump off the cliff, and hope that God will save you from yourself.

To the contrary, risk is calculated, integrated, and then executed with diligence and thoughtfulness. Most people who "left it all," took a risk, and succeeded will tell you that their decision was not flighty or impulsive at all. They made their move only after much preparation and thoughtfulness.

Such a move seems to be a three-step dance.

1. Become aware of whatever is in your heart and "dig it up."

2. Weigh it, deal with it, talk it through, process it, integrate it with your values, judge it, and chew on it until you know with wisdom exactly what you are doing.

3. Take action.

This will keep you from chasing fantasies—the opposite of what the wise déjà vu person does. As Solomon says about that: "He who works his land will have abundant food, but the one who chases fantasies will have his fill of poverty" (Proverbs 28:19).

Sometimes we have impulsive fantasies in our souls as well as treasures. But if we take step two above and talk everything through with those who know us and are there to help us, we can see reality and separate it from fantasy. Chasing fantasies in your heart may be a way of avoiding the real treasures that are there. If Robert had chased the fantasies of his heart as Julia's husband did, he would have ruined his marriage and his life. Instead, he integrated his desires with his values and commitments and found ultimate treasure at home.

Burying Versus Suspending

I think it is important to point out the difference between burying your dreams and simply suspending them. To bury your dreams means to be unaware of them, or to be in some sort of conflict with them. When you bury them, they get stagnant, sick, and begin to die. That is not healthy.

On the other hand, knowing your soul does not mean that you have to realize or accomplish every dream at once.

I know a woman who is raising her three children and truly wants to go to law school. One day she will. She has not buried that dream in any way, shape, or form. In fact, she is looking forward to it. But not today.

She has *suspended* the dream, holding it in the palm of love and sacrifice. She is holding it in her heart along with her other heart's desire: the health and welfare of her children. Step two mentioned earlier dictates that she take care of *all* of her heart, not just one desire. While she desires a law career, she also desires to raise her children well. She puts both desires in perspective with her values and what she knows her children need from her. That is not burying anything. It is holding her desire for a law career on the altar of sacrificial love, which is the highest form of heart and soul that we know in this life. It is the ability to "lay down one's life" for those he or she loves.

No Stagnant Pools

The message from our déjà vu friends is that your heart is an organ designed to have life flowing *through* it. Your mind is like that as well, as is your soul. They are not meant to be stagnant, with things buried in them, stuck there and not moving into the light of the outside world.

But to get to the outside visible world, those desires have to be found, watered, fertilized, and planted. In short, you have to own them, work them, and use them. Here are some tips on how to do that:

- Listen to what bugs you. It might be a message.

- Don't let negative feelings just sit there. Do something about them.

- Don't let long-term wishes and dreams go ignored. Find out what they mean.

- Listen to your symptoms. They might be telling you that you have something to dig up.

- Pay attention to your fantasies. They may be telling you that something is missing that you need to resolve in appropriate ways.

- Face the fears and obstacles that have caused you to bury your treasures.

- Don't confuse envy with desire. You may be envious of someone else's life because you have lost touch with your own.

- Do everything above in the context of your values and your community of people who are committed to guarding your heart. If you do not have such a community, find one and join it.

- Ask God to help you find your heart, mind, soul, and the treasures he has placed there for you.

The message here is that our successful friends do not ignore the little signals that things are not quite right inside. They pay attention to what bugs them, drives their fantasies, delivers stress, or whatever signals make their way up through the weeds to consciousness. Often, the biggest sign that tells us of things buried in the heart is numbness and a life that is not alive. Our déjà vu friends will always choose life, and that means their heart, mind, and soul are always getting attention. And when they see those signs, they take action.

Grasp your dreams. Reach for them. Take appropriate risks. One of the worst things you can die with is potential. Die with failures before you die with potential. Potential is something to be realized, not guarded and protected. So, dig it up! Invest it! And you will find that it is true—life comes from the inside out.

4

PRINCIPLE 2:
PULL THE TOOTH

NANCY ASTOR: *"If I were your wife, I would poison your coffee!"*

WINSTON CHURCHILL: *"And if I were your husband,
I would surely drink it."*

I HAVE A FRIEND I ADMIRE for his character and accomplishments. In fact, he has often done or said things that have contributed to my déjà vu experiences. One of those experiences occurred as he told me the history of his company.

He has been with the company for some time now, and as president he has come to be associated with its success. It is a substantial manufacturing business with annual sales in the hundreds of millions.

But it was not always so. He took over the company several years ago when it was about one-sixteenth the size it eventually became. Although it was nothing then like what he turned it into, it was still a substantial business, with annual profits in the millions of dollars. I am sure that when he became president, others envied him for landing such a good job leading a company that was already successful. All he really had to do in order to be a success was to keep from screwing things up.

The truth is, not only did he not screw things up, he exploded the company in growth. He put it on steroids. Its annual profits became higher than its former total sales. It was quite an accomplishment, and he has become a recognized leader in his industry, receiving many awards for the innovative things he has done. Many now turn to him to learn his business and leadership practices.

One day we were discussing life and how we never really know the long-term picture even though at any given moment we plan as best we can. The discussion turned to how he did not foresee the amazing success he has had. But I pointed out that it did not happen by accident. He had done some things to cause his company to grow like it had, and certainly those things were intentional. I asked him what some of those things were. His answer gave me one of those mystery déjà vu moments that I have experienced when successful people reveal their ways. Here is what he said.

"I sold off 80 percent of the company at big losses when I first took it over."

"What?" I asked. I thought we had been talking about growth—and here he just told me that he ripped through his new company and gave four-fifths of it away! I took math in school, and this just did not add up. *Okay, I have a dollar today, and I think I will give away eighty cents. That leaves me with twenty cents . . . looks like I am on my way now!* That is how it sounded to me. How do you gut a profitable company by giving most of it away at substantial losses, and then expect it to explode?

"Yes, that is right," he said. "I looked at everything the company was doing, and it was making money. But the more I analyzed things, I could see that the *life of the company* was really in about 20 percent of its overall activity. Although the rest of it was okay, I thought it was a drain and a distraction from where the real life of the company was. The real life was in that 20 percent that I decided to keep.

"So, I sold off the rest of the operations and assets, sometimes at pennies on the dollar. I wanted to get them off our plates, out of our hair, out of our lives, and keep them from draining focus, energy, resources, and attention from the good stuff. So, I got rid of all of it. Quickly. And that move enabled us to get focused on the really good things that we had going. And that is what led to our eventual success."

I was having one of those moments. I had seen this before. I had seen successful people let go of very good things that were not the *best* things to them. At that time I did not know exactly how to conceptualize the experience as part of our mystery successful déjà vu person. Later the picture became clear. I now see it all the time in the lives of people who do life well, both in relationships and in reaching their goals.

Principle Two can be described like this:

Successful people do not hang on to bad stuff for long.

Déjà vu people get rid of bad stuff. Period. Sometimes quickly and sometimes through a process, but they get rid of it. They get it out of their hair, off their plate, out of their souls, and out of their lives. They do not allow negative things to take up space in their lives, draining them of energy and resources. If the tooth is infected, they pull it. Immediately. They have little tolerance for nagging pains that are unresolved. They finish off problems and do not allow them to remain. *They get rid of negative energy.*

Sometimes this negative energy is generated by the presence of things that are truly negative, such as a significant unresolved problem. At other times the negative energy comes from things that are not innately bad, but simply are not best for the person involved, as was the case for my friend. You may be involved with things that are not bad in and of themselves but that distract you from those deepest desires in your heart or the most important things in life. Thus they become negative influences draining away energy and attention. As problems go, they may seem to be in the minor leagues. But they can spoil your dreams as readily as the big stuff.

LEVEL ONE: MINOR LEAGUE PROBLEMS

There is a big difference between adequately functioning divisions in a successful company and an infected tooth. On the surface one seems to be a blessing and the other a problem. But, if you lived in my friend's soul, you would see that to him 80 percent of his successful company was an infected tooth. He saw most of the company's divisions as problems in that they were taking away from the things that were important to the future he wanted to build. The bulk of the company was not negative per se; it was profitable. But it was negative in terms of where he was trying to go. So, he pulled the tooth.

Sometimes things are not bad at all in their nature, but they are not profitable. There is no law against them; they just don't do you any good. As the apostle Paul told the Corinthians, " 'Everything is permissible for me'—but not everything is beneficial. 'Everything is permissible for me'—but I will not be mastered by anything"

(1 Corinthians 6:12). He was determined not to let even things that were okay have control of him in any way.

In this passage he was talking about food. But the principle also applies to our time and energy—when we allow anything to dilute our focus. Even though it may not be a bad thing in itself, it may not be beneficial. And if you care about the kind of life you are living and building, then, as it was in my friend's company, things that are not beneficial are problems. They take up time, resources, energy, attention, and do not get you where you want to go. So, déjà vu people dig them up and get rid of them.

While you and I may not be able to relate to a half-billion-dollar business, a simple example of the principle might show up in a review of your cable television bills, as it did when I recently reviewed my own. I had purchased a package that contained several movie channels (not the bad ones!). The package was not expensive, and when I bought it, I thought it was a great idea. With small children, I was no longer getting to the movies regularly, and I missed watching them. The cable package was to be my solution. While the expense was not great, it involved enough money to avoid wasting. (I am a cheapskate by nature.)

As the months went on, I began to realize that I was not watching any of the cable movies. I was investing my time in other ways. Every time I looked at that guide, I would feel something inside bugging me. At first I was in denial and told myself, *Oh, I will watch something soon—when I finish such and such a project.* Then another month would go by and I still had not watched a single movie.

But I was paying for this cable package. It was a drain on my budget every month! It was not a bad thing in and of itself, and I can afford the few dollars it cost, *but it was bringing me no benefit.*

That was bugging me. So I finally changed my plan. I cancelled the movie channels. Out of the depths of denial and into the realms of success! At least in purchasing television viewing packages.

This is not a huge business success story like that of my friend, but the same principle is at work. The reality is that most of life, even big business operations, is done in small decisions much like this.

There are many such examples that we are not even aware of. Clutter, dead weight, things we keep around that don't help us but take up space or drain resources. That is why we need to do periodic spring cleaning in our lives, which is basically level one of this principle. Just as my friend went through the company's balance sheet and I went through my television bill, you probably go through your home, finances, and other areas of life on some regular basis and "clean house." That is normal, and a skill we learn as children. Clean things up periodically. Get rid of the things you are not using. They are taking up space and energy, and costing you at some level.

Maybe you can relate to a few other examples.

- Relationships that you are spending time on that are not going anywhere, or are even taking you places opposite of where you want to go

- Activities that are not getting you where you want to go

- Things you own or are paying for that you are not using, or that are not bringing you true and lasting benefit

- Time you are spending that is not contributing to your real well-being or mission in life

PRINCIPLE 2: PULL THE TOOTH

LEVEL TWO: THE BIG LEAGUES

If level one of this principle is spring cleaning—getting rid of things that are not innately negative but are not profitable—what is level two? Level two is facing things that truly are negative and either fixing them or figuring out that they can't be fixed and letting them go. What I have learned about the successful déjà vu person is that she does it sooner rather than later.

The first of the Nine Things says that the negative things that are buried in a person's heart should not be allowed to remain there. She would bring them into awareness and not permit a cesspool to fester among her resources, bugging her at times, but quickly ignored or denied. She would pay attention to these negative proddings. When my friend looked at the balance sheet of his company and had the thought, *These divisions are not very alive,* he would not allow that fact to be denied, buried, or ignored. He embraced it. Just chewing on the other side or focusing on the positive would not hide the nagging sensitivity of a tooth that hurts.

The second of the Nine Things says *pull the tooth.* Once the negative is discovered, dug up, and brought into the light, it is not allowed any overtime parking. Either the cavity is filled, or the tooth is pulled. Either the broken car is fixed or the tow truck is called. Either the divisions of the company are made vibrant or they are sold off. Either the movie channels are watched or they are cancelled. Then new energy, time, resources, and space becomes available in the heart, mind, and soul to focus on the things that, as my friend said, have *life* in them. The negative energy drain is stopped, making room for the good stuff.

So if level one of this principle is the minor-league spring clean-ing, level two is calling in the repairman or even the exterminator. The major league. Sometimes it is difficult to know when to keep working on something or when to let it go. Later in this book, we will look at helpful ways to make those decisions. But suffice it to say now that the successful person is doing one or the other with anything that is negative. She is either working on it and not allow-ing it to remain negative, or she is realizing that there is no hope and moving on.

You don't necessarily have to get rid of everything that has negative components to it (we would have no friends, marriages, jobs, or anything else of value if we were that perfectionistic). You do have to get rid of the hurtful, negative dynamics of those things. You simply must face and eliminate the drain, the problem of the ongoing, negative energy. That is the point. Stop the insanity!

But sometimes, the negative is not fixable, and you have to give up on repairing something and let it go. That may mean letting go of the expectation that some particular part of something can be improved, or it may mean letting go of the whole thing itself. If you know that investing more time toward reaching a solution is never going to help, then it is time to pull the plug and move on. Forget repairing it or changing it. Let it go.

This principle may mean that you don't throw out a relation-ship because it has certain negative components. Rather, you take steps to get the other person to change some troubling dynamic or behavior. I believe, for example, in the long-term covenant of mar-riage. Marriages should not be torn asunder. But even in such a commitment where you are not going to get rid of the person, there are certain dynamics that you might have to give up on trying to change, at least for a while. Instead, you learn to deal with them appropriately.

For example, if someone close to you has an addiction, and he or she is not changing, you can put an end to that negative poison in *your* life. You can say, "I will not remain around anyone who is not living a sober life. If you choose to continue abusing alcohol, we cannot live together. I have tried to get you to deal with it, and as long as you won't, I can't do this anymore. I am still committed to you and to working this out, but I want us to live apart if you are not going to choose to get help and get sober."

Sometimes, though, relationships and other things do come to an end for a variety of reasons. And that is where many people stall out. They do not know when to repair it or when to end it. As Solomon says, there is a time for both: "a time to search and a time to give up, a time to keep and a time to throw away" (Ecclesiastes 3:6). How do you know the difference? When do you repair a relationship, and when do you let it go? When do you give up on improving a situation, and when do you leave?

We will look at that question a little later in this chapter, but for now, know this: you can only find out by dealing with the problem directly and getting rid of the negative aspect that is damaging your central focus.

You can find out if something is fixable only by getting busy and fixing it.

Question for self: *Are you letting it sit there, or are you dealing with it?*

So, the successful déjà vu person deals with anything that drains time, energy, and resources from the life of those desires and dreams he is working on. When you think about it, this is quite natural. Every baby has built into its hardwiring the ability to embrace things that feel good and are nourishing, and to reject things that are painful or toxic. If something does not taste right, feel good, or hurts, the infant will let you know. He or she will face it, not allowing any space for long.

Even your body is wired this way. Not long ago I went to a restaurant and ordered a glass of milk (one percent, thank you). No one in the kitchen bothered to check the milk's expiration date, which had passed over a month ago. I took a big gulp, and there is no way to explain what that milk tasted like. The experience was beyond taste. As the poison invaded my mouth, nose, senses, throat and being, I made no decision about whether or not to hold on to it. I did not sit there and think, *Hmmm, maybe if I just give it more time it will taste better.* I did not ponder the situation. Instead, my body took over for me. It was involuntary. My entire system rejected the toxic substance. Every muscle group I am aware of was involved. It was automatic—done without a thought.

That is the speed with which our successful déjà vu person's character handles negative things that are in the way of the meal called life. There is a system inside that says almost automatically, *I do not want this in my tummy!* Then it is marked for fix or loss. There is certainly much thought, time, and process put into how to handle a negative situation lovingly and wisely, *but there is little question as to whether or not it is going to be handled.* That is somewhat automatic: it is the very character of our successful déjà vu friend.

Another example is your immune system. Your body is wired with an amazing strategy to fight off the bad stuff that enters on a daily basis. When you breathe, eat, touch, and go through all the experiences of any given day, you come in contact with all sorts of destructive bacteria. When these aliens invade your body, your system does not wait until they have gained more ground and made you sick before it takes action. It instantly sends messengers to find out first what the virus is made of (it seeks to understand it), to mark it as a problem (it puts a little sign up on a cell that says "problem virus") so it can be identified and seen (not hidden), and then it is dealt with—quarantined and destroyed or expelled.

Babies do it, toddlers do it, your body does it. God does it. It seems without a doubt that to get rid of bad things that destroy or weigh down good things is part of the created order. The process is as natural as breathing. And that brings up a very important question:

Why do we stop doing what is so natural?

There are many reasons, but most have to do either with a lack of skills and good modeling of exactly how to acquire and implement an emotional and spiritual immune system, or with fears that come from bad experiences when one has tried to exercise their immunities. Here are some examples you may identify with:

- Fear of someone's anger or hurt if you deal with the problem

- Fear of someone's judgment or disapproval when you deal with negative things

- Fear of actually losing the relationship itself, or at least losing love

- Guilty feelings when you confront someone or deal out consequences

- Experiences with role models who confronted hurtfully, and your determination not to be like them

- A lack of knowledge or skills relating to how to say things, or what to do if confrontation produces conflict, denial, or counterattack

- Paralysis when the problem person comes back at you

- Self-blame and feeling like you are the problem or feeling like you caused it

- Inability to let go of things because you fear that you cannot replace them (you will not find another relationship, job, and so on)

Whether or not you have had difficulty exercising your immune system, you must wake up to the laws of gravity: no matter what your reason is for not getting rid of the negative, if you are going to succeed, you must work it through and gain this skill. I know you may be afraid, and taking the step may be one of the most difficult things you have ever done.

However, your success in relationships and in life is going to be limited or enhanced by how well you exercise these two skills:

1. Your ability to confront and resolve negative things quickly, directly, lovingly, thoroughly, and effectively

2. Your ability to let go and leave behind the things that are not resolvable

PRINCIPLE 2: PULL THE TOOTH

Many people live lives that do not soar because they do not deal with negative drains to begin with, or because they remain stuck in the "fix it" mode longer than is helpful or hopeful. Think of the possible contexts where either of these problems can occur:

- Marriage

- Dating

- Extended family

- Work

- Finances

- Health

- Spirituality

- Neighborhood and community

- Pursuit of dreams and desires

- Possessions

Recently I had a business deal resurface with a problem from a few years back. A lingering debt was owed to me that I thought had been taken care of. My partner in the deal was a long-time friend, but I had never done business with him until this situation arose. I had never had any reason to doubt his integrity or honesty in business dealings. But when I pursued the unpaid debt, I began to see a different side of him.

When I first discovered the debt, I called this friend to see if he knew about it. He had heard about it from our accountant, but he did not believe he owed the money and thus did not bother to address the issue. He said basically that it was not his problem. I told him I would look further into it and get back to him. What stood out to me, however, was that he did not show more concern or take the initiative to actually find out whether he truly owed the money, and if he did, to make it right with me. He just unilaterally decided that it was not his problem and left it in my lap.

At one level, I understood such a response if he was convinced that he did not owe the money. But at another level, I could not imagine treating a business partner or a friend so indifferently. I would want to find out for sure if I had wronged him or owed him, or at least determine how I could help with the situation.

As I dug further into the issue, I found that he did indeed owe me the money. I called him but got no answer. I continued to call for a while, always with no response, and finally I concluded that he was going to blow off the debt and me as well. It turns out that he did resurface and offer some limited help, though the issue is not totally resolved as I write this. But that is not the point. The point is seen in what one of my déjà vu friends said to me.

My déjà vu friend knew the business partner, and I wanted his perspective on what to do next. I told my story and explained that the problem had gone on the better part of a year, and that I was trying to figure out the next step. It would be expensive to get attorneys involved, and there were complicated tax issues that would involve accountants, a lot of time, and a bunch of brain drain. Furthermore, the man was not demonstrating a helpful attitude, and the relational part of the issue was sure to be gross as well.

My friend listened, got all the facts, and said, "This reminds me of a similar situation I experienced years ago. The signs are clearly the same in your situation: your partner is not going to help. Write it off and get on down the road. Take the loss and move on. You are expending too much negative energy."

There was that phrase: *Too much negative energy.*

"Just take the loss and move on? That's it?" I asked.

"Yep. Move on. You don't need all this holding you back, pulling at you for more time, money, and energy than you have already spent. He is not likely to do anything about the debt, and it is not worth the hassle, time, and effort to go after it. Get on to spending your time in ways that will produce something good."

Too much negative energy. I had heard the principle put like that, and I had heard it put in other ways. But the concept was the same: if the problem is not going to be resolved, you have to let it go and put it behind you. Or if resolving it and getting what you want is not going to be worth the cost, you have to let it go and move on. "Know when to hold 'em, know when to fold 'em."

But I could feel my conflict inside. *Let it go? We're talking about a lot of money!* That was not the issue for my wise friend. Whether it was a lot or a little was unimportant. What was important was that no matter what I tried, it was unlikely to work. And if it did, the result would be worth less than I would have to spend to achieve it. Taking into account what I would lose in time, money, energy, creativity, and the love of life, in the end it would be a net negative. Just write it off.

Let it go. Move on. *Pull the tooth.* That is tough to do sometimes, but it is the way of déjà vu people. Otherwise, you are just going to drag that toothache into one more vacation and not enjoy your meals.

THE BRAIN DRAIN

Another troublesome aspect of allowing negative things to continue past their time is the way that the mind deals with them. Think about it. At what moment do you think of the plaguing, avoided, unresolved negative issues from the list on page 55? The answer for most of us: when you can do the least about them. When we avoid facing things directly, they tend to grab us at the times when we cannot address them effectively. For example:

- The drinking problem of a spouse that is not being addressed effectively seems to get the most attention at the family gathering when the person has too much to drink.

- The problem with the boyfriend who is not committing enough to the relationship tends to get addressed in the phone call when he lets you down for the hundredth weekend.

- The character issues of a nineteen-year-old son that have bugged you for years are not faced until he flunks out of college or gets sent home for drug abuse.

- The tax issue you have avoided pops into your mind the moment you lay your head on your pillow to sleep or when you wake up in the middle of the night.

- The debt or interest rate that is not being faced, or the budget that is not being prepared, or the creditors that are not being dealt with, worry you worst when you have to make a crucial financial decision or purchase.

- An acquaintance with people who hurt you consistently is all the more painful as you spend a rare night out with them, and feel the time wasted.

- The tire that needs fixing is on your mind during a drive to an important appointment, with you mentally kicking yourself because you put off the repair.

- An unresolved conflict with a friend or loved one hits you hard when you are away from them, causing crummy feelings that you carry around but do nothing about.

- The health problem you are trying to ignore nags you continually, but not enough to call your doctor today.

- Your tendency to commit to activities you don't like brings up resentment when it's time to attend them, but you don't do anything to get out of them.

- The job you hate but are sticking with for another year when there is no good reason to causes frustration as you drive to work every day.

- Working on a project with that employee that you know you should have fired last year makes you angry.

So, here is the sad result of not living like a déjà vu person: you get the negative emotion of all your problems without the benefit of solving them. Avoidance is really not helping anything, because you still expend the energy and feel the hurt. It may help you avoid the pain of having the tooth pulled, which is time-limited pain, but it does not help you avoid all pain. In fact, you get to endure the problem much longer than if you just faced the hurt of the surgery, dealt with it, and let it go. You could be done by now. Avoidance always prolongs pain, in the end.

One of my déjà vu friends was about to go on an extended trip to Europe. I was having dinner with him a few nights before he left, and I asked how his week had been.

"Really, really good," he said.

"Why? What happened?" I asked.

"I had three tough relationship issues that have been lingering for a while, and I wanted to get them all cleared up before I left. I didn't want them hanging over me while I was away. So, I had several meetings with everyone involved and worked through it all. Some of it was really hard, but it is done. Now I feel that I can take off and really be free and focused." *Déjà vu.*

WHEN TO LET GO

One of the toughest things to figure out is when to let go of something that is important to you. When do you give up hope?

Melanie had fallen pretty hard for Glen. In fact, she was deeply in love with him, and it was no wonder. He was energetic, smart, funny, loving, creative, and possessed a good sense of values. He gave her a lot of attention when they first met, and she thought, as did her friends and family, that he could be "the one." Everybody was crazy about him.

But slowly she began to experience a pattern. It seemed that Glen's work and hobbies took up more of his attention than did she. Sometimes he failed to call when he said he would, and after waiting alone for hours she would just go to bed. She began to doubt herself—her attractiveness, her likability, and whatever else she could question about herself that might explain his lack of responsiveness.

Finally she began to talk to him about the problem. She told him that if they were serious about each other, which both agreed was the case, she needed to feel that she was a priority to him. She felt that she ranked quite low on his list of priorities, even though they had been together for over a year and were talking about marriage. She was not happy with being at the bottom of his list.

Glen was a little defensive, but he agreed to turn things around. And he did so for a while, but it was short-lived. She confronted him with the issue again. She offered to go to counseling. He said he would try to do better, but his "work was so demanding." She was patient.

But after giving him enough time and chances to change, she told him it was over. She broke it off. It was heartbreaking, but with the support of her friends and family, she did it. For a while.

After a month or so, she began to miss the good old days when she and Glen were together and it was so wonderful. She played the scenes over and over in her mind, recalling all of the fine things about him. Why did she break up? Couldn't they make it work? They loved each other so much and had so much in common, it just seemed such a waste not to work it out. She wanted him back.

So she called Glen and said she wanted to get together and try their relationship again. They met and talked, and he agreed to think about it. He missed her too. He promised to call in a day or so. A week went by, and no call. She finally had to call him for a response, and she found him living out his same old commit/no commit pattern right there on the phone.

Melanie came to me and asked what I thought. She said that she had been hoping Glen would change.

"Well, you have to figure out whether there is hope or not," I told her.

"Of course I hope it works," she said.

"I don't know if I would call that hope," I said. "It sounds more like wishing than hoping."

"What's the difference?" she asked.

"A wish is something that you desire and want to come true. You can want it with all of your being. The desire for it can be very, very strong. But it is totally subjective and comes totally from you. It is one-sided and has no basis in reality.

"Hope, on the other hand, is not as subjective. It has objective reasons to believe that good things are going to happen, or at least can happen. For example, if in your time apart, Glen had decided that he has a real problem with getting close and remaining committed, and if he decided to get help to correct that problem, that would be something objective in which to place hope. If he came back and said that he was joining a group of commitment-phobic men, that would be a hopeful sign. If he came back and told you that he realized he must give up his demanding job if he was going to have a serious relationship, that would also be a hopeful sign. But as it is, your 'hope' is really just a one-sided wish with no reason for it to be there other than your wanting it."

"So what should I do?" Melanie asked. It seemed that she was getting the picture.

"Well, I think you should give up hope for the relationship to ever be different," I said, "since there is nothing objective in the picture to say that it will be. In fact, you have over a year of highly objective data telling you it will never be different."

"So, I should walk away?" she asked.

"I did not say that," I replied. "I said you should give up hope for the relationship to be different. Then you can see the reality of what it is. You have data that shows you what being in a relationship with Glen is like and will be like. That is the way it is. That is the way it will be after you have done everything possible to fix it. Now, the question is this: is that what you want in life? Long term, do you want to be number two, or three, or ten on his list of priorities? That is what you must decide, and then you will know whether you want to walk or not. Ask yourself if you like the relationship as it is now, because that is the way it will always be unless you see reason for hope other than 'I miss you and will try to do better.'"

Then for the first time, Melanie reminded me of my déjà vu friends. "I'm done," she said.

Hope is one of the great virtues in life, right up there along with faith and love (1 Corinthians 13). But hope is not a fairy tale wish; it is bedrock, and you should be able to order your life with it at your side. Melanie's initial approach was certainly not a way you would want to order your life, whether you were betting on business or love. Remember that hope means investing time and energy toward results that you have solid reason to believe can be achieved. It is not hope to invest time and energy in a goal that has no forces acting upon it to bring it about. That is stagnation. It is a waste of time, and time is ultimately what your life is about. Pulling the tooth—getting rid of the painful problem—has the added benefit of making room for a positive alternative. In fact:

> *New things that actually have hope for the future*
> *cannot appear until you get rid of what was*
> *taking up the space that the new thing needs.*

If there is no hope for whatever it is you are clinging to, let go of it so you can be open to something new and life-giving.

The Cringe Factor

I hope you are getting the picture that the wise way to live is to put an end to negative things that are using up space, time, energy, and emotions. It is like weeding your garden. It keeps things healthy and alive. But there is another way that the déjà vu person deals with negative problems and energy drains that is even more effective than fixing them or pulling the tooth: *he does not get into them to begin with.*

I went to visit a wise friend and advisor several years ago when I was at a particular juncture in my work, trying to decide from among several options what to do next. We spent a day on a beautiful beach, outlining the possibilities, discussing the people involved, and going over all the pros and cons. One option looked very good and had tremendous potential to accomplish many good things. The only problem was that the person I would be working with was one of those people who has some "issues."

This person is successful, talented, and possesses many other good qualities, but he has a reputation among people he has worked with of making them feel used. When my advisor friend understood that this man was associated with the opportunity, he looked at me and said, "Why would you want to work with *him?*"

I knew what he meant, as I had also dealt with this person previously. I knew the pros and cons. But I had been focusing more on the good things involved in the opportunity. "Well," I said, "that is the downside of the deal. He has a lot of good points, but I have to take kind of a big gulp to think about being connected to him in this deal. I don't like that part of it."

"Let me tell you something," my friend said. "I am old enough now and have enough experience that I just don't do any deal or work with anyone where the *cringe factor* is involved. I just won't do it anymore. I have learned my lesson."

"What is the cringe factor?" I asked.

"That is the big gulp you would have to take to go forward," he explained. "My rule is this: anytime I have to cringe or take a big gulp to agree to do anything substantial with anyone, whether to hire him, work with him, or anything significant, I don't do it. I won't go forward as long as the cringe factor is there. Period."

My mind left the beach for a moment. I immediately went back to a time three years ago when I had entered into a horrible business situation because I had ignored the cringe factor. I had gone forward in a very good deal involving a person that I had to take a big gulp to work with. It turned out to be a nightmare. I wished at that moment I had followed my friend's advice three years earlier. I understood what he was talking about, and the cringe factor has become a guiding principle for me ever since. And because I heeded this advice, I am not tethered to the person we were discussing, and that means I have no tooth to pull.

So the lesson here is that the best way to fix a problem is not to have it to begin with. Learn to listen to that little voice inside that tells you things like:

- *This doesn't quite feel right.*

- *I really don't feel comfortable doing this or agreeing to this.*

- *This is not what I really want.*

- *I don't like what I am agreeing to.*

- *This violates an important value.*

- *I am going to resent this tomorrow.*

- *I am going to resent this for a long time.*

- *I wish this were not happening.*

- *This feels the same as the last time.*

Solomon gives us a great proverb about the cringe factor: "A prudent man sees danger and takes refuge, but the simple keep going and suffer for it" (Proverbs 22:3).

If you encounter a situation that you would not want to live with, fix it before you go forward, or don't go forward without realizing what Melanie had to realize: you are choosing to live with that tooth. You had better have a very good reason to choose such a course. The best way, like my wise friend says, is to not go forward. Don't be like the simple or naïve who keep going and suffer for it. Because you will suffer. How much you will suffer depends on how bad the tooth is. The best way to fix a problem is to not have one to begin with. An ounce of prevention is worth one million pounds of cure.

When your senses tell you that something is wrong, there is a reason you feel that way. Check it out and see if it is paranoia or wrongful suspiciousness on your part first. If it is, work through it.

But if it is not, listen to it. It will save you from bad relationships, bad business deals, bad purchases, bad debt, hurtful situations and circumstances, bad choices, and many other negatives that your life will be a lot better without. Resist the impulse to say yes.

Make the Appointment

In summary, my déjà vu friends would give you one piece of advice about your aching tooth. Make the appointment. Pull the tooth. Deal with whatever is wrong. That may mean fixing it, or it may mean getting rid of it altogether.

The overriding principle is that unresolved negative things are a drain and take away from that which has life. They have no place in your heart. That principle does not negate patience, longsuffering, hope, or working out difficult relationships over time. It includes all of those things, doing whatever you can to fix what is wrong and make it better. Forgive and reconcile. But it also means not to let bad situations sit, stagnate, get infected, and drain away your life. "A cheerful heart is good medicine, but a crushed spirit dries up the bones" (Proverbs 17:22). Move quickly to deal with whatever is crushing your spirit. *Déjà vu.*

5

PRINCIPLE 3:
PLAY THE MOVIE

The day shall not be up so soon as I, to try the fair adventure of tomorrow.

—SHAKESPEARE

THE OLD MAN SAT DOWN on his favorite bench, settling in with his newspaper for his lunchtime ritual. He was a man of routine and could be found here most any day, enjoying the trees, the children playing, and the sounds of the bustling city around the park.

One day a young man sat down next to him with a paper of his own. The old man moved over a bit to make room, and went back to reading.

After a few minutes, however, the new bench partner said, "Excuse me, sir?"

"Yes?" the old man answered, looking up with a friendly smile.

"Would you happen to have the time?" the younger asked.

The old man looked the young man over for a moment, taking in the fact that he was pleasant looking. "No," he said, then went back to reading his paper.

Puzzled, the younger man could not imagine why the older

man would not give him the time, having noticed that he was wearing a watch. So, he asked.

"Umm, excuse me, sir?"

"Yes?" the older one replied.

"I don't mean to be a pest here, but I am curious about something," said the younger. "I can't help but notice that you are wearing a watch. Yet, when I asked you if you had the time, you said no. Have I offended you in some way?"

The old man just looked at him, not saying anything for a moment, but eyeing him up and down. Finally, he said, "No, not at all. You seem to be a nice enough young man." Then he went back to reading his paper.

This seemed ever more strange to the young man, so he persisted. "Then I don't understand. Why won't you give me the time?"

The older one put his paper down.

"Well, when you first sat down, I noticed you. You seemed like a nice enough young man, clean-cut and all. You seemed interested in the world and its current events, as I noticed by the particular paper you were reading. That was impressive. Then you asked me for the time. And I figured if I gave it to you, we might strike up a conversation. And if we started a conversation, you would probably tell me about yourself, and I would probably like you and we would become friends.

"And if we became friends, I would see you here again, and we would get to know each other better. Then, I would probably invite you to my house sometime to meet my family. If that happened, you would meet my wonderful daughter whom I love very much. With you being such a nice young man, she would probably like you. And, as beautiful and wonderful as she is, you would probably like her too. So, the two of you would probably get to be friends, and go out on a date. And if that happened, chances are you would fall in love and get married. And I'll be hanged if I am going to allow my daughter to marry any man who doesn't own a watch!"

GOING TO THE MOVIES

Déjà vu people rarely take any action without considering its future implications. Tell a man the time and you might just end up marrying off your daughter to a guy who doesn't own a watch. Life is a slippery slope!

You never know exactly what might happen on down the line when you make any given choice, but the wise person at least thinks about it. However, what I began to notice about successful people is that they do not just think about future implications when making those big, scary decisions. Almost everyone does that. Déjà vu people tend to think that way all the time, in matters large and small.

So here, then, is the third of the Nine Things I've seen my déjà vu friends use to be successful. We've seen that we must dig up and invest our talents, and move past the negative. Now we see that successful people know how each scene contributes to the film's good end.

There are several ways to think about Principle Three. The simplest is to look at it merely as a matter of cause and effect. "If I do A, then B will happen." That may be the easiest way, but it doesn't illustrate the profound nature of it. Experience takes us much farther than that. It's more like this: *If I do A, not only will B happen, but C will too. And D and F and G and so on and on.*

That is the difference between the simple law of cause and effect and the deeper version of true sowing and reaping. Sowing and reaping is much bigger than the immediate connection between what I am doing now and what will occur immediately following. Sowing and reaping is about what I will *ultimately* end up with (take in, live with, be stuck with, and so on) if I sow this particular behavior, choice, attitude, value, or strategy. It is the long-term view. More accurately, it is the end view. *What will happen in the end?* is the question the wise person seeks to answer.

Successful people evaluate almost everything they do in this way. They see every behavior as a link in a larger chain, a step in a direction that has a destination. And they see this link in both possible directions, the good *and* the bad. They think this way to attain the good things that they want in life, and they think this way to avoid the bad things that they do not want. In short, they rarely do anything without thinking of its ultimate consequence. They play the movie, so to speak.

Playing the movie means never to see any individual action as a singular thing in and of itself:

Any one thing you do is only a scene in a larger movie.
To understand that action, you have to play it out
all the way to the end of the movie.

After viewing the entire film, you can decide whether you really want a particular scene in the movie of your life. If it alters the plot or your story, or takes you to other scenes that you do not want to live out, or even causes the movie itself to have a different ending than you had plotted, then you do not want it. No matter how inviting the scene itself is, you do not want it.

Conversely, if it alters the plot of your story in a direction that you *would* want to go; if it creates later scenes that you would want to live out, then you might indeed want to add that scene. No matter how hard the scene itself is, you might want to choose it.

Play now, pay later. Pay now, play later. We teach this to six-year-olds. How much better our adult lives would be if we would always live it out ourselves.

The Future Will Come

Once while I was doing a seminar on reaching goals and dreams, a lady asked if we could talk for a moment. We sat down and she told me her story.

"Ever since I was a little girl I have had this dream of being a lawyer," she said. "I used to watch TV shows about lawyers; I read books about trials; I even used to go watch trials being conducted at the courthouse. I would love to practice law. It would be the ideal profession for me. I would love the work, and it would also be a great way of helping people."

"What do you do now?" I asked.

"I work in the loan industry," she replied.

"How do you like what you are doing?" I asked.

Her face changed to a cross between revulsion and hopelessness. "I hate it," she admitted. "Every day I wish I were doing something different, especially practicing law."

"Well, sounds pretty clear to me. Why don't you do it?" I asked.

"Because it would take too long to get there," she said.

I asked her what she meant.

"Well, obviously I would have to go to law school, and that would just take too long," she said.

"How long would it take?" I asked, wondering if I was missing something. Usually law school takes about three years, which didn't seem like a long time to me when one was thinking about a lifetime of work. (Having gone to graduate school for five years myself, I may have been simply trying to get revenge.)

"It would take about three years," she said, confirming my estimate.

"And you hate what you are doing now?" I repeated.

"Yes. I mean, I love the people I work with, and I am grateful for having a good job. But it is just not how I want to spend my life," she explained. "But, it would take too long to get my law degree. So, I feel a little stuck."

It was clear to me that she did not know how to *play the movie.* So I played it for her. "Let me give you something to think about," I said. "Do you plan to be alive three years from now?" I said.

"Well, I should certainly hope so!" she replied.

"Okay, then think about this. That date is coming. Period. It is not optional. Three years from now will come, and you will be alive. I repeat, *The three years is not optional. It is going to come and pass. You will be here,*" I emphasized. "Now, here is the question. Since that day is going to come three years from now, on that day do you want to have a law degree, enabling you to do something you love? Or do you want to be still hating your life?"

She just looked at me.

"Before you answer, let me emphasize what I just said," I continued. "You said the reason that you have not chosen to go to law school is that it would take too long, as if the passing of three years were optional. But three years are going to pass. That day three years from now will be here. It is not an option. The question is what do you want your life to look like on that day?"

"I never thought about it that way," she said. "It is not about three years seeming like a long time. It is about where I will be in three years if I don't do this . . ."

Now she was catching on to the script of the movie. She could see that her choosing to avoid school was not just an isolated decision. It was only one scene, but the movie was going to keep playing regardless, and that scene would dictate the way it turned out. The movie is not optional, but where its plotline goes is. She could choose to be in a very different movie, one that she would like. Or she could choose to be in one that she did not like at all. It was up to her.

The thing to remember about the sequential nature of life is that the passing of time is not a choice. Three years would take too long, she said. Well, *too long* is coming, period. You don't have a say in that. But you do have a say in what your life will look like when *too long* gets here.

When we think of a difficult thing to do, like attending graduate school or changing careers, we often just think of the immediate comfort that comes from not doing it. No, *I won't do it* gives a little relief from the big gulp of work that school would be for three years. But, that is a big lie we tell ourselves—a lie that hides the future consequences of our choices. Yes, you avoid the work. That feels good at the moment. But in doing that, you have made another choice as well: *to have a life you hate three years from now.*

We act as if the present is all there is; we forget that the future is going to come either way. Immediate relief from hard work is not the only consequence. By avoiding the immediate discomfort, you also sign up for the negative consequence residing within the future reality.

Two Sides of the Same Coin

Wise people play the movie to prevent negative things happening as well as increase positive things in life. And by doing so, they can change behavior that they would not otherwise be likely to change.

Bill was an example of this. He was in his late forties and gaining more and more weight. He had tried many diets to little avail. He would begin them well, but soon he would lose motivation and get off track. Usually he gained back more weight than he lost. It had become a destructive cycle. Now more than a hundred pounds overweight, he had basically given up.

While talking to him, I learned a frightening fact. When Bill's father was about his age, he collapsed and died with heart problems brought on by obesity. Bill not only had a clear health risk due to his weight, he also inherited genes which made that risk even greater. I asked him what he wanted to do about it, and his answer gave me little hope.

He said he knew that he had to lose weight. Although he had never before followed through on his diet and exercise program, he said he was going to get more committed this time and stick with it. He was determined. This time it would be different, he was sure.

But I played the movie. It was a rerun. He had tried many times before to do what he was vowing to do now, and it always ended the same. I could see him trying to "will-power" himself to turn away from delicious cheeseburgers and exercise. But it just was not going to work, no matter how much commitment he invested. He did not possess what it would take to do it.

Nevertheless, his answer was that he was going to be more self-disciplined than in the past. So, I asked him, "Who is going to be more self-disciplined?"

"I am," he said.

"But your history shows that you are essentially undisciplined. How is an undisciplined person going to become more disciplined? Are you the problem or the answer? You do not possess the discipline to do this, so how can you expect to be what you are not? That is like my telling a car with an empty tank to get more gas. It cannot do it," I said.

Bill looked at me with an expression that was a combination of knowing the truth and realizing that the truth is not good. He knew that if he were honest, he just could not do what he was asking himself to do. It is a depressing moment. "So, what do I do if I can't do it?" he asked.

"Well, you are in a good place, actually. You have come to the end of yourself, and that is usually when a person truly gets better. When you face the fact that you are powerless, then you look outside yourself to find the power to do what you are unable to do. That is how people usually change, and it works," I said.

I explained to him that he had not lost weight because he could not make himself do what was necessary to lose it. He did not have the structure, discipline, or self-control to pull it off. In addition, he was probably using food to medicate himself against a lot of hurt, stress, and other negatives. So the answer was to add the discipline he needed from the outside.

He would have to join a structured program that would provide the structure he did not possess. He would need a group to work on his hurts and the things that he was running from, as well as to support him and be a team with him. He would need a buddy or two he could call when things got tough. Also, I told him he had to learn to ask God to help him in moments of temptation as well. And I told him that if he stuck to a regimen of this kind, he would lose the weight. It would be statistically rare for such an approach not to work if he stayed with it. I had seen the proper recipe of support and structure work for too many people.

But there was another problem, one that only playing the movie could solve. As the old saying tells us, *the program works if you work the program.* I knew that *the program* would work, but I did not know if *Bill* would work it. What was lacking was the motivation to remain connected to the program. It was time to get him to play the movie.

Bill had young children. So I asked him to write several scenarios that begin with his dropping dead tomorrow of a heart attack. I asked him to write the stories of his children's lives starting tomorrow without a father. First, see them at the funeral. Then watch them grow up without a dad to help them develop their values and negotiate the difficult teen years. Write the stories of adolescent girls looking for male attention to fill the void of not having a father and show how that vulnerability might affect the choices they made with guys.

Then I asked him to think about where his family would have to live without him as the breadwinner. What about their loss of friends and community when they were forced to move after his death? What kind of atmosphere would their next neighborhood provide? How well would they live on what his wife could earn? What opportunities would they lose to make their dreams become reality? And what kind of discipline would they muster to achieve those goals without a father's guidance?

Next, I wanted him to write his wife's story as well. How would her life play out after losing her husband at such a young age? He needed to include the struggle of finding herself in her late forties with young children, with no real marketable skills since she had devoted her career to motherhood and then having to go to work to provide for the family. How would her working affect the children? They would not only lose Bill; they would lose a lot of her as well. Then watch the movie of her empty-nesting alone. Or worse, marrying someone she did not love just for the security.

Then I asked Bill if that movie might help him stay connected to the plan that would help him succeed. "I get it," he said. "I cannot let that story come true. I cannot do that to them. I will not let it happen."

Playing the movie was the turning point for Bill. Remember, it was not the answer. Just playing the movie would not empower him to quit binging and start working out every day. But it did provide the motivation to hook up with the things that would empower him. He needed a lot of help, and the movie motivated him to get it. (This is similar to what occurs with an alcoholic who goes to Alcoholics Anonymous meetings to help stay sober. The program and the support network are what enables him to succeed. But playing the movie of what drinking has done to his life and will continue to do is what motivates him to work the program.)

Going to the movies can save your life by preventing bad things from happening, and it can build your life by enabling you to see the good things that can happen. I have a friend who devotes a certain amount of his spare time (not all of it, which is wise too) to buying and fixing up rental properties. This is not as much fun as other things he could be doing with those free weekends, for sure. So what keeps him out there on those Saturdays? He told me that he plays the movie ten to fifteen years down the road. The mortgages will be almost paid off, the rents will have increased, and he will be retired. I am sure that he has to play this movie each time he faces a choice between going fishing or going out to look for one more fixer-upper. But at the end of the movie, he is doing a lot of fishing and golfing and not a lot of working!

HELP ALONG THE WAY

In addition to motivation, playing the movie provides successful people with another strategy common to all of them. They use it to live out the difficulties before they actually occur. They "borrow trouble," in a way quite different from worry. *Don't borrow trouble from tomorrow by worrying* is good advice, because it is a bad kind of debt. It is borrowing with no pay off. Worry is often the non-acceptance of situations that you cannot do anything about. People who worry about things they cannot control would do well to learn and practice the Serenity Prayer: "God grant me the serenity to accept the things I cannot change, the courage to change the things I can, and the wisdom to know the difference."

But successful people often borrow trouble in a way that can give a payoff. They borrow trouble from tomorrow in situations that they *can* do something about. They worry ahead of time—

they play the movie—and then they take active steps to make sure they are ready when that scene arrives.

I had lunch one day with a déjà vu friend who owns a highly successful construction company. "What are you working on now?" I asked.

"War games," he said.

"What?" I asked.

"We are having a week of what we call war games," he replied.

I had to ask. Surely he had not gone back into the National Guard.

"We play out future bad scenarios and make sure that we are in a position to handle them. For example, right now interest rates are at a certain percent. What does our company look like two years from now if the rates go up a point and a half? What if land costs increase? What if, at the same time, there is a union strike? Then we look at what that would do to us and whether we would survive. Since those are real things that happen, we make changes in how we are structured so that if or when they occur, we will do well in spite of them."

That is being a lot more active about the future than just making sure you have enough cash reserves, isn't it? No wonder this man has been so successful for so long. He will thrive in the tough times because he has already lived through them, theoretically, and survived.

When I conduct seminars on reaching goals, I often have people isolate and plan the worst things they will have to face if they try to reach their goals. I have them play the movie ahead of time and devise a strategy to prepare for the worst scene before it hits.

For example, if a man wants to build a new career in sales, he will have to make cold calls. When he looks at the past movies of his attempts at cold calls, there is one scene that always changes the outcome of the movie. He runs into a few rejections, gets very discouraged, becomes fearful of making more calls. He retreats into his old, safe routine that will not get him where he wants to go.

So I have my seminar participants plan on that scene. We do an exercise where the bad thing just happened. They are rejected and feel horrible. It is time to make another call and take another risk.

"How do you feel?" I ask.

"Terrible!" they say.

"What do you want to do?"

"Quit," they say. "Give up."

"Okay," I tell them, "now that critical scene is coming up where you are feeling discouraged enough to quit and give up, and you have to make your next cold call. What are you going to do?"

Then they make a plan. Call their buddy, form a support group, get with other people who are trying to make it, pray—the list goes on. They build strategies that prepare them ahead of time for the failure that has derailed them in the past. And this time they do not fear it. *They are expecting it.* It is coming. They are counting on it. And they are preparing for it. They have seen the previews. And this time, they will know exactly what to do.

I have a friend who was a porn addict, though he has been "clean and sober" for some time. He said that for him, breaking free required discovering this concept of "triggers," the event that began his cycle of isolation, withdrawal, depression, and then finally porn use. That would be followed by guilt and shame, and the cycle would begin again. He found that the entire cycle would always begin with some personal interaction in which he felt he was put down in some way. That was the trigger.

When he learned to play the movie forward, he was ready. For example, if he had a meeting with a higher-up in the company who had a harsh personality, he would play the movie and see the upcoming scene where he would feel put down. Then he was ready. He knew what to do. He had a sponsor in his recovery program prepared for a call, both before the meeting and after. He also had a Twelve Step meeting he could go to. Eventually, after being ready for those scenes and successfully negotiating them, the triggers lost their power. He was so successful in dealing with them that other people lost their ability to make him feel put down, even when they tried. He had found the power of self-control. All from playing the movie and being prepared for the difficult scenes. Playing the movie ahead of the triggering crisis enabled him to seek help to keep the crisis from spinning him into his destructive behavior.

The same was true for Sarah. She was caught in a tough cycle while trying to break up with a boyfriend who was no good for her. She had ended the relationship several times, but each time she found the loneliness and depression too great to bear. She would decide to go back to him, at least for a while, to end the pain of loneliness. But it would not be long before the same patterns would trigger the need to break up again. She could not sustain the "getting over it" time period.

So Sarah and I played forward the movie "Going Back to Him When I Am Depressed" past the planned break-up. This time she was planning ahead for her depression, loneliness, and feelings of abandonment. Therefore, when that scene occurred, she knew what to do. She assembled a support network, which kept that show running in front of her at all times. They met regularly and were on call for her when she hit the lows. She revived her spiritual life. It all worked, and she is now free and married to a much better man! She is the star of a much better movie as a result of playing the difficult scenes ahead of time. Déjà vu.

BIG THINGS, SMALL THINGS

We've been talking about major life decisions and challenges. But déjà vu people live out the principles of success in the small things of life as diligently as in the big things. They do not play the movie only to deal with major crises such as potential heart attacks or losses of relationships. They play it to handle the details as well. It is just the way that they operate in life. Period. Remember, big wins are usually a collection of very small steps. For instance:

"I would love to watch that TV special. How will I feel at work tomorrow if I stay up that late?"

"I want to buy that dress. It would make me feel good now, but how will I feel when I pay the Visa bill next month?"

"I want to stop by and see Marsha . . . but if I do that, it will rush me to get that report done before dinner. And if I don't finish it before dinner, I'll have to do it afterward, which means missing time with the kids. I'll have to see Marsha another time."

"It is only September . . . I have a lot of time left for Christmas shopping. But last year I hated Christmas because I spent the whole week before running around like a chicken with its head cut off finding gifts. It was too stressful. I don't want that again. I am going shopping today."

"I want to buy that new couch, but I promised myself I would get my savings up to a year's expenses before making any new purchases. If I buy this, I will not meet my savings goal."

These examples seem like small things, and they are. But the way of handling them is not small at all. It is one of the most powerful ways of success that there is. And the déjà vu person follows it in the small things as well as the large ones.

PLAYING THE MOVIE IN DIFFERENT CONTEXTS

Playing the movie applies in every area of life. Let's look at some examples.

Relationships

In the middle of an argument, a person is tempted to blow off steam and become sarcastic or cutting. *But,* he asks himself, *where will this go if I say that?* Venting may feel good for the moment, but he can play the movie ahead and know that it will be all downhill if he says what might feel good at the moment.

In dating, when a woman is not sure where she wants a relationship to go, she can play out the implications of saying yes to things that are being asked of her. *If I go on this trip, what will I have communicated to this person? How far will I be into something that I am not sure I want to be in?"* A man can ask himself, *If I kiss this person, what have I implied? What expectations am I setting up?*

When a difficult person makes a request and you say no, he gets angry and manipulative. You immediately feel the pressure to cave in to his demands. It would get rid of the immediate conflict and relieve the pressure. He would turn into that nice person you enjoy as long as you are saying yes. It is tempting to give in to keep the peace. But you take a moment to play the movie and realize that if you do cave in, what you are saying yes to is going to totally mess up your calendar, or your time, or your heart. And that is going to take you way past the moment of today. In addition, by giving in you have trained that person one more time in how to get his way with you. Proverbs 19:19 tells us not to rescue an angry man, for "you will have to do it again." Give in to the tantrum in this movie scene, and you have lost whatever you were trying to hold on to. And you have continued in the same old plot for the future.

In a marriage where you face control, rage, disrespect, addiction or other character problems, you check your gut and ask how it feels to be passive and not take a stand. You sit there and experience all the negative fallout from the problem, and then you look down the road one year, two years, thirty years, and realize that if you do not confront the issue and become an agent of change, this is the future you can count on, or worse.

You become aware that you have very little time for your spouse or children because of the career situation you are in. You leave before everyone wakes up and return after the day is way past done. Basically, you never see your family. And, this is not merely for a season, as it is for a tax accountant in April. It is the way the entire program works. Play the movie and you will see that because you have not built your relationship with your spouse well, you have begun to drift apart. Your children grow up on their own and really do not know who you are. Other people are forming their personalities and character, not you. You picture them as teens drifting into counterculture because they are alienated from their parents.

PRINCIPLE 3: PLAY THE MOVIE

Parenting

Your child blows off cleaning up after himself in the kitchen or den. You have told him that he must finish his chores before playing. But it is late, you are tired, and you do not really have the energy to discipline. You just want to have a moment to read, and the mess is not a big deal for you. Play the movie. See your son at twenty-five, married, and leaving that mess for his wife. Day after day, he expects her to take care of his responsibilities in life.

Or, your daughter snaps at you and is disrespectful. Play the movie and you will see the tone and nature of her relationships in the future when she does not get her way. Or, you say no to her and she cries her way into a yes. Play the movie and you can see what her husband and friends will be in for, as well as how she will be resented instead of being loved and appreciated.

Your child does something annoying. You get angry, and raise your voice or snap at him to get him to behave. It works . . . for the moment. Play the movie and see him trying to make it in life with fear and guilt as his constant companion, or with a broken spirit. See him attracted to difficult, angry people as a result of how his parent modeled relationships. See him living his life trying to achieve the impossible goal of always striving to keep difficult, angry people happy.

You are tired at the end of the workday. But your child has not seen you all day and comes up to you wanting attention. It is so easy to tell her to watch a video or go out and play. You are busy. Play the movie, and if this is a pattern, see her learning that she is not desirable or worthy of anyone's attention. See her attracted to detached and emotionally unavailable people, trying to get love that is not available. Picture all the destruction that comes from that.

(Okay, if you are codependent, and usually are responsive to your child, don't go eat a carton of ice cream right now to escape the guilt this example is causing. You deserve some time for yourself. I am talking about someone who would push away their children frequently, creating a pattern that the child is internalizing.)

Here, this next example should make you feel better: You are normally very attentive to your child, even today. And you have been so attentive that you have had no time for yourself. Your child still wants to play even as you sit down for a moment to yourself. You feel that you ought to put down your book and accommodate her. But you play the movie and see a bleak future for your daughter. She is a demanding slob who cannot stand to give people the space or time for themselves that they need. (There. Does that get rid of your guilt feelings?)

You had it very hard growing up, and do not want your children to have to work as hard as you did. So you give them a generous allowance and shower them with opportunities to enjoy life, sports, and fun activities. You give them the childhood that you never had. You are glad that they do not have to provide for themselves at fourteen, and you are grateful that you can buy them clothes and the finer things of life. There is nothing wrong with that. But if you are giving them no counterbalancing responsibility, play the movie and see what they look like at thirty if they do not learn to work and earn some of what they need. They still live at home, borrow from you, resent their jobs, and soon leave them.

Your child is upset about some misunderstanding with a friend he was playing with. He runs inside crying. You hate to see him upset. Instead of sitting down, talking it out, and pushing him to go back and work it out with his friend, you feel sorry for him. You know he loves ice cream, so you give him a couple of scoops of vanilla with chocolate topping to make him feel better. He cheers up, takes the bowl, and settles in front of the television. Things are better now. Or are they? Play the movie to the scene where he is older, seventy-five pounds overweight, afraid of arguments, and withdraws into TV and computers instead of establishing relationships where he might have to work out conflict.

Morality

You are married, but you find a certain man you work with attractive and attentive. You slowly begin to spend more and more time around him at work, and eventually the two of you find ways to spend time together outside the office. Those meetings have no legitimate business connection. You begin to fantasize about what it would be like to be with him sexually.

Stop and play the movie. Watch the upcoming scenes where you see yourself as a duplicitous person, looking your husband in the eye and lying. Play it forward further. Watch the scene where he finds out, which usually happens, and see him—and a few friends and your parents—confronting you. Look at your children's faces as they find out that their home is coming to an end. Look at your life as a divorced person—two homes for the children, complicated single issues, and the "wonderful" other man who is now back with his wife. Or if he is with you, look at the lack of trust you have for this person you met in an affair, a proven cheater. See your fantasy as the first scene of a tragic story if you choose to live it out.

Or, your tax burden is more than you can afford this year. You see opportunities to claim items as expenses that are not really business related. You consider turning in receipts for goods and services from sources that you truly did use, such as taxis, restaurants, suppliers and vendors, contractors, and equipment companies, but that are not real business expenses. It all adds up to cover your tax shortfall. Your problem is solved and no one will be the wiser.

Play the movie forward and see yourself looking your boss in the eye as he thinks you are a trustworthy employee. Look at your trusting wife who thinks you take care of finances in a way that enables her to sleep at night. Look at yourself feeling like a crook and a cheat. Then play the scene where you open a letter from the IRS explaining that you have been selected for a random audit. Or more likely, that one of the companies you expensed is getting audited, and your account is part of their audit. As the scene continues, they find your padded reports, turn you in to your boss, and by policy, even though he likes you, he must fire you. The IRS presses charges against you as well. Your accounts are attached. You now cannot pay your mortgage and you have no job. Fast forward to the scene where you try to get a job as a felon—or as someone who was fired for stealing from the company. Then come back to the scene you are considering playing out into a reality. Compare the immediate relief of your tax problem to the direction the movie of your life will take if you siphon off that small amount of money that no one would miss.

PRINCIPLE 3: PLAY THE MOVIE

Health

In Bill's example earlier, we saw how the movie can play itself out to help you see where certain health habits are headed. Here are a few more suggestions.

Attach a picture of a cancerous lung to your cigarette lighter. See the movie depicting the grueling course of cancer treatment—if you are lucky enough that your cancer can be treated.

Take a picture of yourself in your current shape and put it on the refrigerator you raid for between-meal snacks, or on the alarm clock you set to get you up for your workout. The picture should help you to set your alarm and leave the refrigerator door alone. Or, if you find it more motivating, use an old picture that shows what you want to look like again.

See yourself at older ages, unable to move about because of diabetes, heart problems, joint problems, or whatever. See your family missing time with you and you missing time with them as they engage in activities you would love if you had the health and energy to do them. Play the scene showing the pain of all the health problems associated with lack of exercise and poor diet. Find pictures that depict these problems and post them in places that will remind you when you are making those choices. If you use a system of calorie or point counters, associate your diligence in sticking to the program with real outcomes as you play the movie forward.

Play the movie of your wife's emotions. Get inside them and see what it feels like for her to be with a loved one who is not taking care of himself. See the disappointment that she feels in you. Feel what it is like when it becomes difficult for her to be attracted to you because you have disregarded your health. See the fantasies that she sometimes uses to overcome how she feels inside.

Play the movie forward, as Bill did, to show the result of just deciding that you are going to do better at your health but without doing anything other than making the same old commitment you have made many times before. Play the movie forward to see your future if you fail to get outside help from buddies, a group, a system, a structure, or some sort of treatment with support from a weight loss community. Look at the research that promises statistical failure if you try it on your own.

Then think about all the people who make it if they work the program instead of trying to do it on their own. Plan for the moments when you are ready to drop out of a program because you "have tried that before." This time plot a movie that includes the scene of your quitting your smoking or overeating, and get the right supporting actors involved in that scene.

And my favorite example of playing the movie forward in regard to healthy habits: *A moment on the lips, forever on the hips!* Now that is a bad movie.

NOT ALL MOVIES ARE BAD

We have spent quite a bit of time playing bad movies in this chapter. But remember, as we showed above, for every bad movie that follows a pivotal scene, there is a good one that can follow if that scene is re-scripted. You saw the tragic movie scripts I had people write if they included the bad scenes they were about to live. But I also had them write scripts with happy endings that would come about if that scene were rewritten. Bill wrote the scene of giving his daughters away at their weddings because he was healthy enough to live to see that day. The woman who wanted to be an attorney created a whole picture of what her life was going to look like when that third year in law school ended and she got her degree. It seems that with human nature being as it is, we need a lot of reminders on the negative side. But I want to bring you back to the positive so that you will *play the movie* to choose the immediate scenes that will bring about the ending you desire.

One of the best examples of this procedure is Tiger Woods, who grew up with Jack Nicklaus' major tournament record pasted to the headboard of his bed. It was the first thing he saw every morning when he woke up and the last thing he saw at night. He was playing the movie of his future, winning more major tournaments than the king of golf. Long before he ever played in a major tournament, he had been playing the movie of himself *becoming* the next king of golf. And now we are seeing that movie unwind as a reality right before our eyes.

Think about this: how many times do you think Tiger Woods was tempted to sleep an hour longer instead of getting up before dawn to hit practice balls before school? How many times do you think he was tempted to add a more attractive scene to his movie that would have him partying with friends rather than practicing two more hours on his putting? I am sure that such temptations were countless. But at those moments he knew that none of those immediate scenes would take him to the end of the movie that was posted on his headboard.

ON THE BIG SCREEN

Plot a movie, a vision of your starring character, your relationships, your spiritual life, your career, your health, your finances. See it, plan it, and then evaluate each scene you write every day in light of where the movie is supposed to end. If you do that, and make sure that you include the right supporting cast along the way, I will be so happy for you when you get your Oscar for a life well lived. "Well done, good and faithful servant!" (Matthew 25:21).

And the cool thing is that the accolade is not even the best reward. The best reward is the life itself, the life you have built over time. That is the reality that will not only last for eternity, but will also give you abundance and fulfillment along the way. Choose the right scene at each pivotal moment, and you'll be the star in a great movie. One scene at a time.

6

PRINCIPLE 4:
DO SOMETHING

There are no passengers on spaceship earth.
We are all crew.

—MARSHALL MCLUHAN

W HY ARE YOU looking at me like that?" Gretchen asked.
"Like what?" I asked. "Like I am supposed to do something about it," she said.

It was one of those moments in which I wondered whether
mind-reading truly was possible or she was just a lucky guesser. I
really *was* thinking that she should do something. However, I was
not trying to look as though I thought that. I was just listening to
her. Actually I was trying to do nothing and let her think it out for
herself. She was the kind of client who always wanted someone
to tell her what to do. Then when she was told, she was as likely to
resist the advice as to take it. I had learned this about her early in
her counseling and had refused to play the game anymore. But I
had to be honest.

"Well, now that you ask, that is what I was thinking," I admitted,
a little annoyed that I was so transparent.

"What do you think I should do?" she pressed.

"I did not say that I was thinking of what you should do," I said. "I just agreed that I was thinking you ought to do *something*."

"Do what?" she demanded.

"Something," I said.

"But *what*? How in the world could you be thinking I should do something when *something* was not even anything," she said, somewhat contemptuously. "Something is something, not nothing."

"That is a fair question," I replied. "Let me explain. It is like what a friend of mine said to her seven-year-old son when he came to her and wanted her to fix the fact that he was bored. He was sitting around the house with no friends and did not like having nothing to do. So she told him, 'Daniel, you are responsible for your own fun. So go find something to do that you enjoy.'

"That is kind of what I was thinking in this situation with your sister Jean," I told Gretchen. (Jean wasn't speaking to Gretchen because of something Gretchen had done.) "I was not thinking of *what* you should do. But like my friend with her son, I was thinking that if you don't like the way things are, then it is up to you to do *something*. You are responsible for your own "fun," and in this situation you are certainly not having any. So I thought you should do something about that. *What* you do is a different question."

She shifted in her chair, and I continued.

"Your central problem is that whenever anything is wrong in your life—whether in a relationship like this one with Jean, or at work, or in your social life—you always think that the solution to making it better is going to come from the outside, not from you. The answer for you is the same as for that bored kid: fun is not a bird that is going to land on your head. But a better relationship with Jean is not going to show up at your door through her initiative. Fixing the next step in your career is not going to come in the mail, and neither is the man of your dreams. Yet you always expect that someone else is going to make the first move to create the solution. And if they do not, you stay stuck in the problem, resentful and wishing life were treating you better."

I said I could sit there and think she should do something because I believe that is what people who succeed do. They *do something instead of nothing.*

"So when you think that I believe you should do something, you are right. But I was not thinking about what you were to do at all. I was just noticing that it is your move."

"But," Gretchen protested, "she is the one who is bugged with me. I didn't do anything to her. And if she has a problem with me, it is her responsibility to come to me. I didn't cause this. It's her problem."

"True, she is bugged, and she should come to you," I said. "But, as I have listened to you, you sound bugged too."

"Yeah, but only because she is bugged with me," Gretchen retorted. "That's what bugs me. She is causing this. So it is her responsibility."

"But when you are bugged, whose *bugged* is it?" I asked.

"What do you mean, whose bugged is it?" she asked, slightly exasperated.

"Just what I said. When *you* are bugged, when that feeling is inside of *you,* whose gut is that feeling lurking in at the moment? When you are bugged, whose bugged is that?" I persisted.

"Well, mine, I guess. But I didn't cause it."

"I did not ask who caused it. That only matters to a judge in a court if you decide to sue someone. If it rains, you did not cause that either, but it is your head that gets soaked if you don't come in out of the rain or open an umbrella. So in a thunderstorm, are you going to just stand there, get wet, be miserable, and say, 'God caused this, so it is his problem. He should make the first move'?"

It just did not occur to Gretchen that there might be something she could do to make the situation better, whether someone else does anything or not. Now if she had asked what I was thinking at that moment, I would have told her that I was wondering how many times I would have to have this conversation with her until she got it.

The repetitive conversation had to continue until she did get it, though. That is how important I believe this issue is. It is the fourth of the Nine Things successful people do in love and life. Principle Four says:

Déjà vu people ask themselves the question:
What can I do to make this situation better?

Déjà vu people have a certain quality. In addition to listening to their heart's desire, getting rid of negative stuff, and thinking of how the present will affect the future, they do something else. They tend to call on themselves as the first source to correct difficult situations. *It does not matter whether they think they are to blame or not.* Even if someone else is at fault, they will ask themselves, *What can I do to make things better?* The answer might be to call the other person and deal with the issue, or even to try to get him to take responsibility for his fault. Or the answer may be to call someone else for help. It could be a number of things. But whatever the answer, *they make a move.*

PRINCIPLE 4: DO SOMETHING

ARE YOU DRIVING YOUR LIFE,
OR JUST ALONG FOR THE RIDE?

Proactivity

There are many different ways to look at this principle of *making your move*. For many years psychologists and philosophers have talked about related dynamics. For example, you may have heard some people referred to as *proactive*. That term usually refers to men and women who take positive, initiating steps in life as opposed to merely reacting to situations. They do not see themselves as victims of people and circumstances but as active participants who take steps to influence outcomes. If there is a problem in life, the world, or themselves, they do something to solve it. If they want a situation to be better, they see themselves as part of the solution, or at least as a catalyst to get it going.

Locus of Control

Another psychological perspective on this subject is called *locus of control*. That term refers to where a person perceives the "place" of control of himself lies. In other words, are you controlled from outside yourself, or inside? In Gretchen's case, she had distressing feelings of being "bugged," as we called it. Where was the locus of control of those feelings? Did all hope of her feeling better lie outside of herself or inside? Could she do nothing but sit and wait for relief to come through her sister calling and expressing a change of heart? Or would Gretchen have felt better if she took control and called her sister first?

Dependency

Still another psychological way to look at this principle is in terms of *dependency*. People who are overly dependent or approach life with an attitude of dependence tend to be less successful than their counterparts. This does not mean that to depend on others is a bad thing, for that is of itself a measure of emotional health. We need to be able to depend on other people because we all need each other. The problem comes when the dependency is passive and we look to others to do what we should be doing ourselves. To put it simply, I should not depend on another person to do my job.

Gretchen was taking a dependent stance. Should Jean have come to her? Of course. But Jean's failure to take the initiative is Jean's problem. Gretchen's problem was that she would not do her own job of taking the initiative to get herself "unbugged." She was not asking herself what she could do to resolve her own feelings and repair the breach in the relationship. She was depending on her sister to do it for her.

In light of the above ways of looking at the principle of this chapter, Gretchen was 1) not being proactive; 2) placing the control of herself outside of herself; and 3) depending on her sister to make the situation better. No wonder she was bugged!

With that pattern, I was not about to have a déjà vu experience with her. The situation did remind me, however, of one of my déjà vu friends. I saw him on a weekend, and while we were catching up I asked what his upcoming week looked like. He said, "It is going to be tough. I have some hard relationship issues I have to *face into*."

Face into... now that is an interesting phrase, I thought. That is not a figure of speech; that is how he does life. He *faces into it*. It is active, not passive. Going toward life, not away from it. He leans toward it and propels himself into it.

It was another déjà vu experience for me. In none of his life did this friend wait for the solution to come and find him. He went and found the solution. He turned his face toward the situation and leaned into it. The mental picture I got was of track runners leaning over the start line waiting for the gun to fire. He was leaning toward the goal, eager to be let loose to make the situation better. Even when he was facing into something negative, he did not hold back or turn away. It is one thing to face into making vacation plans but quite another to face into tough relationship issues. He was being proactive, taking control of what he could control (himself), and not sitting back depending on someone else to make it all go away. He was going to *make his move* to do what *he* could do to make it better, regardless of the other people involved.

But, having confronted many people and urged them to take such active steps, I can tell you the common response: *But what if they. . . .* Whatever the issue, when you press non–déjà vu people to get active and do what they can do, they respond as if what they should do depends on what the other person does. Usually they say something like, *But what if they don't listen?* Or, worse, *They will never listen,* as if they know the future they have never tried to effect.

I have never seen successful people stall out because of some feared, anticipated, or hypothetical outcome. They just do not think that way. They do what they can and then deal with that outcome just like they dealt with the issue in the first place. They get active and *face into it* all over again. Unless there is some good reason to believe that making a move is not wise, they do *something*. And by the way, waiting and not making a move *is* making a move if you are strategically waiting with good reason. Déjà vu people wait as well as act, not because of passivity or fear, but because they have a purpose.

Ownership and Responsibility

Psychologists are not the only ones who have noticed this dynamic. Philosophers have talked about it for centuries, as have theologians and spiritual guides. The philosophical category that it most often falls into is *responsibility.*

This is not the kind of responsibility that you think of in terms of "doing your duties." We often think of being responsible as equivalent to taking out the trash or doing your taxes on time. That kind of responsible means that we do what we are supposed to do or perform the task that is placed before us.

Philosophical and psychological responsibility, or *existential responsibility* as it is called, means much more than that. It means that you and I are responsible not just for duties or jobs, but also for our entire existence. For example, you are not only responsible for taking out the trash, but also for being in the situation which includes taking out the trash, for how you feel about taking out the trash, and for choosing not to do all the other things you could be doing instead of taking it out. If you do not like taking out the trash, that is your problem, not the problem of whoever you think is making you do it. If you agree to perform the task, then it is your responsibility. Not your fault, maybe, but your responsibility.

To psychologists, philosophers, and theologians, who is at fault, is not the big issue. That is a legal question. What is an issue is being responsible in terms of *ownership.* To own my life means that it is mine and no other person's. I can blame no one for what I do with it. I can blame them for what they do to me, but *I cannot blame them for what I do with what they do to me.* I am responsible for how I respond. Gretchen could blame her sister for being bugged with what Gretchen did or said. But she could not blame Jean for her own feelings of being bugged at the fact that her sister was bugged. She had to own the fact that her own feelings were her responsibility. Those feelings are in *her* life, in *her* skin, in *her* soul, not in her sister's.

This owning of our lives is similar to owning other things. If you own your car, then you are responsible for it. If you own it, then you also control it. It is yours and yours only. You can paint it, you can put in a new engine, you can set it on fire, you can let it rust, or you can do whatever you want. It is yours. It is under your control.

When placed in Gretchen's situation, people who own their lives would take control of their feelings and have a different experience than hers. How they respond is totally up to them. Some would get angry and go yell at Jean. Others would go out and get the rest of the family to join them against Jean, seeking revenge and causing dissension. Some would not be too affected by the experience and would feel pity for Jean because of her petty, limiting attitude.

Others would get on the phone and call Jean. They would seek to understand the roots of the breach and try to communicate a desire to reconcile and forgive. Others would desire to be loving and mature, but find themselves unable to be anything but angry. Yet they would choose to get help with their angry feelings so they could acquire the strength to choose better reactions than anger. On and on we could go with endless possibilities of both good and bad ways of handling the problem.

The point is that there are a number of possible responses, and we are free to decide which direction to go. We might even find ourselves unable to be all we want to be at that moment, but we can be someone who wants to take steps in a better direction. For example, we may want to be a person who could face Jean with courage, but we do not have any. But we still want to be a person who can acquire courage, so we take steps to become that person.

Addicts who take ownership of their addiction do this every day. They cannot do any better, *but they can do better at handling not being able to do any better.* They get help. Responsibility and ownership means that we have to take control, even of being out of control. No blame, no victims. Unable, but responsible for their inability. Winners take the cards they are dealt and play them well.

At seminars I often ask attendees whose fault it would be if I left the seminar, walked outside, and got hit by a drunk driver. Everyone understands that it is the drunk driver's fault. But, whose *responsibility* is it to go to rehab and get my broken legs back into shape? Who has to take ownership of that disability? That disability is not my fault; I did not cause it. And the courts would agree about the legal question of fault. But it is my existential responsibility to deal with my life and to work at improving it, no matter how adversely it has been affected. No one can do that for me, although they can help.

We all need help at times. God helps, and other people help. But we must do our part as well. Philippians 2:12-13 tells us to "work out your salvation with fear and trembling, for it is God who works in you to will and to act according to his good purpose." We have to do our part while others are doing their part to help us.

Underlying all déjà vu people is a strong sense of personal ownership and responsibility. None of them needs to be told, "It is your life." They already know that and live accordingly. In a sense it would be correct to say that they cannot do otherwise. I have never seen a successful person who did not think this way.

The Gift of Freedom

Ownership and responsibility may sound like onerous terms. Isn't life supposed to be fun? Sure. You are even hardwired that way. You have brain chemicals that help you feel good. And few things feel better than freedom. So, how does one find freedom? That is the good news that follows the "bad news" of ownership and responsibility.

Freedom is the fruit that grows from the soil of these words. As Epictetus said, "No man is free who is not master of himself." Think of how wonderful it would be to gain freedom in:

- Relationships

- Finances

- Morality

- Spirituality

- Feelings

- Choices

- Attitudes

- Emotional Reactions

- Career

- Stress

- Addictions

- Guilt

Life gets fun when we begin to feel free to live it. But there is no freedom apart from responsibility and ownership. Think of a house. You are not free to do what you want with it unless you own it, or own the rights to it through a lease. And since we can't really be mere guests in our own lives, ownership and responsibility are the only paths to freedom. When we stick to these paths and gain freedom, life becomes a joyous experience.

Your Move in Action

We live out our lives in various contexts, circumstance, and environments. At any given moment we find ourselves in many roles and relationships. While contexts change, the constant is who we are as people, our character, and how we express that character in the ways we live. The déjà vu person tends to be consistent in living out the *get moving* approach in whatever setting he finds himself. In many different contexts, he applies the three principles we looked at earlier—proactivity, internal locus of control, and nondependency. As a result, he practices ownership and responsibility, and therefore finds freedom.

What Making a Move Looks Like

When there is a breach in a relationship, as we saw in the case of Gretchen, the déjà vu person figures out what she can do to repair it. Instead of hoping that her sister will make the first move, a déjà vu Gretchen might take the following actions as appropriate:

- Ask, is there anything in my attitudes or actions that have contributed to this problem? What can I do to change those?

- Deal with my hurt and anger so my communication is more likely to help things rather than hurt.

- Ask, how can I communicate to the other person that I see the role I have played in our problem?

- Go and apologize.

- Go and confront.

- Go with an agenda of only listening and trying to understand how the other person has been hurt.

- Go to make amends.

- Get feedback from others on what ways I need to change, and find out how to do it.

With difficult people who are hurtful, angry, controlling, or have problems that affect you negatively, instead of letting your feelings be dependent on their moods or behaviors, *do something:*

- Go and make them aware of the problem.

- Ask if there is anything that you can do to make it better.

- Set limits on your exposure to the problem, and let them know that you will not be around them as long as it is occurring.

- Offer to help them get help.

- Bring in others to help; perform an intervention of some sort.

- Get away if they are abusive, and say you will not be around until they get help.

- Leave the room if they lose their temper, and tell them you will be glad to talk when they calm down.

- Take responsibility inside yourself for your reactions and the way that you allow them to get to you.

- Choose different and better reactions than the ways that you have responded previously.

- Get help to respond differently.

- Manage your expectations.

- Love them instead of expecting things from them.

- Stop enabling the problem in whatever way that you do.

- Do not depend on them for things they cannot give, such as approval, validation, or love.

- Enforce consequences.

With a dating life that is not working:

- Ask what you could do to meet new or different kinds of people.

- Ask the people who know you what there is about you that may be contributing to things not working out.

- If you are consistently attracting, or attracted to, a certain type of person, find out how you are causing that to happen.

- If meeting new people is a high goal of yours and you live in a place where that is not happening, take responsibility for that fact and do something that will help.

- Join a dating service.

- Deal with dependencies that are making you come across as desperate and needy.

- See a counselor about your issues that are contributing to the problem.

- Call former boyfriends or girlfriends and interview them about why it did not work and what they think you could change.

- Deal with dependencies that render you unable to say no to the wrong kinds of people.

- Get your long-term goals and values in line with the choices you are making; for example, if you want someone spiritual, don't go after more shallow attributes and allow that to be okay.

- Let your friends and network know to think of you if they meet someone who might be compatible.

- Get out and get involved in activities that would expose you to new people who like what you like.

- Get over your fears of making the first move and asking someone out.

- Deal with your narrow categories that are ruling out potential dates by being too picky or having some type that you are looking for.

- Be open to going out with people that you would not consider as possibilities for long-term relationships, just to learn, grow, and have fun.

- Value friendship as much as romance.

- See if your values and your behavior match.

- Look at your dating history for patterns and issues that you need to resolve.

- Get honest about your physical appearance and take ownership for how that might be limiting your chances.

- Do the same thing with your personality or habits.

Compare the people who actively do the things in these examples with the ones who sit and complain, stuck in their misery and wishing that someone in particular or life in general were treating them differently. I have seen lives transformed when people begin to adopt the déjà vu person's strategy of asking himself, *What can I do to make this better?*

Miracles have occurred. I recently attended the wedding of a woman who had complained to me a couple of years ago saying, "I wish I were married, but God just has not chosen that for me at this point in my life."

She passively blamed her single status entirely on God. It never occurred to her that she might do something to help him. She was going nowhere that would enable her to meet new people. And she was burdened with so many relational issues and fears that even if the right guy did come along, her baggage would have prevented her from establishing a healthy relationship. And she was being very passive in her approach to making herself available.

I challenged this woman to take responsibility and be proactive. God would help her, but she needed to give him a little cooperation. I showed her many verses in the Bible making it clear that she was responsible for doing her part in this situation. I then challenged her to allow me to be her dating coach. She was hardheaded enough to take me up on it, and I introduced her to this *get moving* strategy. I told her that she had to do whatever I asked her to do, and of course I promised that it would not be illegal, immoral, or unethical. But if she expected her situation to change, she would have to take some active steps toward seeing things as her move.

The end of the story is that after going three years without a date before we implemented the *get moving* strategy, she established a significant relationship within six months after adopting it. She learned meaningful new relational skills from that relationship, and then shortly thereafter, met the man she married. Here is the exciting fact: she had been stagnant in her dating life for longer than it took to get moving and get married.

Just as the parable of the talents tells us, when you are burying yourself in the ground, not making your move, time will pass with absolutely nothing happening. She could have been stuck for twenty more years had she not gotten active. If you have been stuck in ways similar to this woman, her story should get you pumped to get active and make your move.

Recently I was talking to a friend, Tony Thomopoulos, who became president of ABC Television. The story of how his career got started is a great example of how to be an active participant in the events that shape one's life.

He began in the proverbial mailroom. Think of that; right out of school and stuck in the basement of a big conglomerate. But his signing on as a mail clerk was an intentional move. He chose the mailroom over other more interesting positions because he knew that delivering mail throughout the company would put him in contact with every department. He would meet all the people in the company, know what they did, understand all the jobs, and then be better equipped to work his way up.

He then set a goal to be involved in a certain division by a certain date. He did not limit himself to some narrow description of a job, but agreed with himself to take any position available just to get in that division. To show how actively he was thinking about the *"my move"* strategy, he promised himself that if he had not made it into that division by his goal date he would leave the company and seek his career elsewhere. The heat was on for him to be active—pressure imposed by no one other than himself.

Through delivering the mail, he met employees in human resources and learned of one weird opportunity coming up in his targeted division. Someone was needed to take over a position for just two weeks while an employee was on vacation. The hours, 4:30 to 8:30 in the morning, were such that he could take the temporary position and still keep his regular job.

He knew nothing about the work he would be doing in the temporary position, but that didn't stop him. He spent the weekend researching how he could do the best job possible in the short two weeks that he would be in that division. He arrived each morning at 3:30, an hour early, to prepare for his tasks. He also studied his boss, learning his needs and the things that would make his job easier. He found ways to benefit his boss instead of just trying to make himself look good. He truly served his boss. He added value.

After two weeks, the boss was so impressed with how prepared Tony was and the job he was doing that he hired him away from the mailroom. My friend was now in the division of the company that he desired. From there he was picked up by the upper management, and the ball started rolling that placed him in the president's chair a handful of years later.

Luck? Providence? Certainly. As Tony said, "I can see that God was involved in every step." But it was the same God who gave us the parable of the talents. That story tells us that God's system requires a successful person to behave exactly as my friend Tony did.

Did you ever notice that to get to the Promised Land the Jewish people had to travel, fight wars, and cross a river? God provides for the birds of the air (Matthew 6:26), but have you ever seen one that did not leave the nest when it grew able to fly? Does God drop mosquitoes into the bird nest? Not hardly. He provides bugs for flying birds that go out and seek them.

Dig up your dream, but then ask yourself, *What do I need to do now? How can I improve my lot? What do I need to do to get where I want to be? What skills do I need to develop? What fears do I need to get past? Who do I need to meet? How can I invest my talent?* Those questions address steps toward proactive initiative, which God's system demands of those who expect success. Then he asks us to ask him for his provision to open doors and make opportunities for that initiative to be exercised. We must pray, he says, and *we must also act.*

Think of the other guys down in the mailroom or even of others in positions at higher levels than Tony who would go home every night and say to their wives, "This company is a joke. They don't see how much value I bring. There are just no opportunities to move up. Those stupid managers don't know what they are doing." Like my client who couldn't find a date and blamed God for it, these complainers get stuck because they do not ask themselves, *What do I need to do to make it better?* They are not proactive, and do not realize that they could take control at least of themselves. Instead they passively wish that God, life, or management will do it all for them. That is not how you become president of a major company, or even get a date.

If it takes money to make money (a common excuse), then go raise the money. Do not sit there and say, "Gee, if we had some ham, we could have some ham and eggs if we had some eggs." *Do something. Make a move.*

If the economy is lousy, do not wait for it to change. Gain a skill in a different field, look somewhere else, find another niche that is hot, enlarge your network or openness to other jobs, start your own service business, or *something.* Do not just sit around and wait.

Do not wait for your kids to show you respect; move towards them and find out where their heart is and where the breach has occurred between you and them. Find out why they act disrespectfully. Get into their world; do not require them to come over to yours. Yours may be really boring. Stand up to their disrespect with good boundaries and require different behavior. And if you don't know how, get help.

Do not wait for your depression just to go away. Make an appointment for help. Learn about the illness—what causes it and what heals it. Join a group for support and treatment. Go to recovery, every day if you have to. See a doctor to determine whether you need medicine. Monitor your thinking. Read books. Develop your spiritual life. But remember, it is your depression (or anxiety, or fears, or addiction) and it is your move, at least to reach out for help.

If your child is going through a stage in which she is being difficult, don't wait for the stage to end on its own. Engage the child where she is, while she is in that mood, and do what you can do to help her negotiate it. Do not expect from your child a level of maturity that she does not possess. You are the parent. Be the big person.

If you are lonely, do not wait for the phone to ring. Get out and find someone. And if you are afraid to do that, join a support group that helps people get unafraid. If that is too scary, see a counselor who helps people get strong enough to join a support group that helps people get unafraid.

As the great British actress Dame Flora Robson said, "Ask God's blessing on your work. But don't ask him to do it for you."

The Created Order

I believe that God created the earth and all that is in it, and then he created us. He created us in his image, and we were designed to do basically the things that he does, just in much smaller measures. We are designed to dream up new things, be creative, work hard, rest, celebrate, know things, make choices, love each other, and do all sorts of things that He does. We are to act like him; that is what it means to be in his image or likeness.

He still does his part today, and we are to do ours. He provides the resources, and we are to use them. He places us in our own Eden, although it is now an imperfect one, and we are supposed to use the resources of our environment and our nature to reflect his image. We are to be loving and fruitful, as he is. We are to be productive, and like him, we are always to ask how we can contribute to making every situation better. Whatever relationship, job, family, city, or church we find ourselves in, we are to be working to redeem it, bringing light and healing into darkness and sickness.

God did not put us on the earth to fail to reflect his likeness. We turn our backs on his purpose for creating us if we do not reflect his nature. He did not intend for us to be misfits. He did not plan for us to sit back and allow life to follow the course of least resistance, becoming miserable, oppressive, unjust, full of mistakes, unloving, poverty stricken, ugly, lazy, negative, and evil without moving to do something about it. Such passivity is as far from reflecting the image of God as one could imagine. To the degree that we allow life just to happen and are not active forces to change whatever situation we find ourselves in, we are not living up to our true humanity by reflecting God's nature. And that may be the reason you are stuck and not getting to where you want to be.

So get with the program! Be who God created you to be. Get active. You can rest on the seventh day, but do not sleep the whole week long. Reflect the image of the One who created you to be productive with the seeds that he provides: sow them, plant them, work the garden, and then realize a crop in your life. That is the way that he made things to work, and that is the way that St. Déjà vu would do it. In being proactive, déjà vu people become not only good and faithful servants, but also very fulfilled in love and life as well. Get moving and *do something!*

7

PRINCIPLE 5:
ACT LIKE AN ANT

When you have a great and difficult task, something perhaps almost impossible, if you only work a little at a time, every day a little, suddenly the work will finish itself.

—ISAK DINESEN

IT HAS BEEN SAID that if you want to be successful in something, then watch those who do that thing well. That is good advice, and I try my best to follow it. So far my déjà vu friends have taught me that life comes from within, and do not hang on to negative stuff. They think of how actions affect the future and ask how they can make things better. But little would I have guessed just who (or what) would show me the fifth of the Nine Things we need to follow to be successful. I'll explain.

There was a point in my life when I faced what seemed to be a very difficult task, and I really did not know how I was going to accomplish it. It seemed that I was being asked to leap over the Empire State Building flat-footed.

The task was to write a doctoral dissertation to complete a Ph.D. degree. In my defense, lest you think I am the only flake out there who would think such a task was difficult, there are many people who find it overwhelming. In fact, quite a large number of people go through three to four years of graduate school, complete all the coursework, and end up being A.B.D.s (all but dissertation). They never get their doctoral degrees because they cannot complete a dissertation. I could have been one of them.

Not finishing a degree does not make sense for someone who had always done quite well in school, as I had, until you look at the nature of the work. Most grades are achieved through classroom performance, where there is a lot of structure. You have a teacher breathing down your neck, regular assignments, a schedule, a class that meets at a certain time, papers due on certain dates, and a test or two along the way.

A dissertation is quite a different animal. There are no classes, no assignments, no papers due, no one telling you how to do it or structuring the task as you work on it. There is just this monstrous requirement with its own rules and an end date three or four years out from the time that you finish your classes. The due date itself provides little pressure because it is so "out there" that at the beginning it feels like time is not even an issue. It is easy to tell yourself, *I have plenty of time.* And many people find out the hard way that time runs out. (This actually is a pretty good metaphor for many people's dreams in life. Since there is no course helping them get it done, "someday I will" provides temporary relief, but time runs out and the dream is never fulfilled.)

So here I was, looking at this task which involved choosing a topic, researching all the pertinent literature that exists on it, coming up with some question or angle on that topic that has never been addressed before, writing an experimental design that will prove the answer to a significant question or hypothesis, finding the appropriate statistical proofs for that purpose, designing a method to gather all the data that will prove that hypothesis, finding human subjects to participate in the experiment who are a good fit, running the experiment itself, designing the instruments to measure the construct, gathering the data, calculating the results, interpreting them in light of your original hypothesis, making conclusions about the results, integrating those conclusions into existing literature, and then suggesting what would be helpful further study.

If you think that is a difficult paragraph to read, think of trying to accomplish these tasks with a personality makeup that does not think in modes that fit the demands of the process.

I was the kind of person, at that time, who just did not think in terms of sequential tasks without structure. I had no problem with work and study—I always got my work done—but I was not good at developing a structured program on my own to accomplish the many and varied tasks that a dissertation required. Now, many years and over fifteen books later, I am a lot better and actually find unstructured, self-disciplined tasks like writing books enjoyable. (Who says that people cannot change? So take heart!)

But back at the time of my dissertation, the very thought of tackling such a monumental project was so overwhelming that I did not know where to start. So I did what I had learned to do whenever I don't know what to do: I prayed. I asked God to help me, because I knew I did not have a chance of getting this thing done on my own. At some point I was led to open my Bible. Here is what I found:

> *Go to the ant, you sluggard;*
> *consider its ways and be wise!*
> *It has no commander,*
> *no overseer or ruler,*

yet it stores its provisions in summer
and gathers its food at harvest.
—PROVERBS 6:6–8

I looked at the passage again, wondering how in the world this was going to help me with my dissertation. I noticed the word *slug-gard,* which means "indolent." I looked it up: "1 a : causing little or no pain; 2 a : averse to activity, effort, or movement: habitually lazy; 2 b : conducing to or encouraging laziness" (Webster).

Thinking that God was trying to tell me something, I pondered the definitions. At first I could make no sense out of them. Causing pain? What did that have to do with it? As to the second, I did not see myself as someone who was averse to activity or effort as I had always been extremely active. I was not lazy. I came back, though, to the first definition and began to see the point. My tendency was to choose paths that caused me little or no pain. In this situation, I was avoiding the pain of tackling the dissertation because the task was too overwhelming. It was so painful even to think about that mostly I didn't! So I could accept that much as being true about me.

Then I considered the part of the scriptural passage about watching ants. Ants? Watch them? I always just sprayed them. Then as I reread it, the passage got quite interesting. The ant, it said, had no commander, overseer, or ruler—no teacher—standing over it, yet it gets its "dissertation" done by harvest time. Hmmm. That was exactly my problem. I had no boss giving me orders, and I was not getting it done on my own.

I did not know where to start figuring out how to apply what the scripture was telling me, so I decided to do exactly what it said. I would watch the ant and learn.

PRINCIPLE 5: ACT LIKE AN ANT

Where do you watch ants? I didn't know. I could have solved the problem by leaving a few brownies on the coffee table, but somehow that did not seem quite the way to go. Then a friend bought me an ant farm. I felt a little silly, as most ant farms are probably purchased for eight-year-old kids, but I set up the glass container, and after the ants came in the mail, I poured them in.

They seemed pretty sleepy from the trip, so not much happened at first. When I looked in on the ants later, they had shaken off their jet lag and were busy as—well—ants. Each of them had one little tiny grain of sand in its grasp and was marching from one end of the little green terrarium to the other. I had no idea what they were doing with those grains, but they were marching somewhere with them, one by one. Okay, I thought, this is interesting but it does not seem to be adding up to getting a dissertation done.

I was away for a few days, and when I came back something had happened. The sand between the panes of glass was beginning to take some sort of shape. It had been moved around into clumps, and little tunnels were beginning to form under the surface. But when you looked at any given ant, it carried just one little grain of sand. *The activity of any individual ant seemed to have little impact. Nor was it apparent how any single grain had much to do with the big picture of what was forming.* But the impact was happening, and form was developing.

Of course, you can guess what happened so I will fast forward. A little more time passed and an entire ant city had been built. It had hills and valleys and a complex network of tunnels, which was amazing. It looked like a team of architects and construction crews had been there for months with miniature bulldozers, trucks, and cranes.

The reality was that many tiny ants had taken many tiny steps— one step at a time, one grain of sand at a time, one day at a time. And voila! A city was built. It hit me and hit me hard. *This entire amazing feat was really no more complex than one ant with one pebble. One step at a time, one grain at a time.* Suddenly it became clear how to get a dissertation done: one grain of sand at a time; one brick at a time; one step at a time. If the ant could do it, I could too.

I began to think about what the grains of sand were for me. The big dissertation was a mountain and impossible to build. But what if I built it in grains, one at a time? I began to break the mountain into little grains, each small enough for me to carry. Grain one: Call someone about a topic I had in mind for researching. Okay, I could do that. Grain two: Meet with him and get his input. Okay, we could do lunch. Grain three: Go to the library and do a search on the topic. Yes, that was a grain of sand I had lifted many times in two decades of school. Grain four: Call my research teacher and ask him what design he would suggest for the dissertation. Yes, I can do that. Grain five: Meet with him . . . okay. And so on. . . . I began to think like the ant.

Could one lonely ant build a city? No, not if you think only about the task as a whole. No more than I could do a dissertation. But the ant could pick up a grain of sand and walk across the terrarium, and I could do little stuff like make a phone call, go to lunch or the library. So I picked up the phone and carried one grain of sand.

Not too long after that, one grain at a time, a dissertation appeared in my hands. What seemed impossible for me had been done. How? Just like Henry Ford said: "Nothing is particularly hard if you divide it into small jobs."

PRINCIPLE 5: ACT LIKE AN ANT

IT IS ALL SMALL

What those ants taught me was one of the most important principles I ever learned, and one that successful people follow all the time in love and life. What was still hidden from me at the time, though, was that very fact. I did not know that this was how all successful people accomplished what they did! I thought it was a technique used to unstick people who could not seem to get things done. I thought it was a lesson for people like me at that time, people who found a task impossible that seemed easy for others.

I looked around at other people who had written doctoral dissertations, and it seemed so easy for them that I thought I was the only one who did it the ant's way. The rest of them probably dashed off the whole thing in an afternoon. I "knew" that was true just as I knew that people who had wonderful marriages fell instantly in love and lived happily ever after and that wealthy people just had a knack for money. It was easy for them—they just did it. Like those guys at the beach with all those muscles that I didn't have. Probably born with them. That was just how successful people were—successful. Some had it and others did not.

If I had examined the few significant accomplishments I had already accomplished in life, I would have seen that *they were done in the fashion of the ant as well.* But I didn't. We don't tend to see such things in our own lives. We look at what we cannot do, or have not done, and somehow think other people are endowed with something special, not remembering that our own successes may cause us to appear that way to others.

It took some déjà vu friends to bring this point home to me. It was certainly a way of doing things that they all embraced and practiced. They all achieved their successes through Principle Five—by acting like an ant.

They achieved their goals by taking tiny steps over time.

BUT, I WANT IT ALL . . .

I was talking to a non–déjà vu client, Jessica, one day about her weight. Frustrated about her dating life, she had decided, again, to lose weight. She had about thirty pounds to go.

"What is your plan?" I asked.

"Well," she said confidently, "I am just going to go for it. This time I am motivated in a much better way. I want to do it for me and my goals instead of feeling like I am giving in to some man's demands."

Jessica had a pattern of resisting getting into shape after a bad experience with a man who had valued her for her body. Her way of rebelling was through ice cream independence, which said, *You are going to have to love me just like I am or you can't have me at all!* Unfortunately, even though unconditional love is an essential in life, unconditional approval of her weight did not seem to be coming forth. She realized that she was going to have to give up her demanding stance, get in shape, and accept the fact that a healthy body would make her more attractive. (She needed to learn to pick men who would value more than just her looks. Her choice of men, however, is another issue. The issue before us was how to lose the weight.)

Jessica continued, "I don't want to mess around. I found a liquid diet that my friend used, and she lost twenty-five pounds really fast. I am so psyched up for this; it really feels different this time."

I was a little hesitant to rain on her parade. But for her sake, I had to. "Didn't you do that once before?" I asked.

"Do what, that diet?" she asked. "No, I have never tried that one."

"No, not the diet. Didn't you lose weight quickly before? Like a lot of weight?" I asked.

"Yes, a few times," she said. "But when Reese played his game on me, I just ballooned back up. I am stronger now."

"That is what I was afraid of. You think the only reason you gained the weight back was the dynamics with Reese and the unconditional love thing. I don't believe that," I said.

"You don't believe that I rebelled against his demand for Skinny Minnie?" she asked. "How can you say that? We really worked on that a lot."

"Oh, I believe that you rebelled against his demand," I said. "But I don't believe that is the only reason you gained the weight back. I believe it involved a couple of other things as well."

"What?" she asked.

"I think it was two things. First, your life did not change, only your weight did. You lost the weight, but at that time you were not growing inwardly and you did not add to your life the kinds of habits, structures, support, and the like that goes with successful weight loss. You just lost weight, but did not change your life. Weight comes from life, not the other way around. Now you have your life ordered much better, and if you integrated all of those structures into your weight-loss program, you would have a much better chance of not gaining it back.

"But, there is also something else, Jessica," I continued. "I believe in the research, and basically to keep weight off you have to make a lifestyle change and maintain it steadily. It is not about dumping a bunch of weight. It is about changing your life, meaning not only reducing your intake and increasing physical activity, but also keeping those changes going over the long haul, a little bit at a time, each and every day.

"If you lose a bunch of weight fast without changing your life, it is going to come back. But if you focus on changing your habits and allow the weight loss to be a slow result of a truly changed life, then it is going to remain off. A small amount of exercise every day, small cutbacks in calories or points or whatever you are counting, and a small amount of oversight and accountability with others each day and an increased amount every week or so. What that translates to is a pound or two per week, coming from very small steps."

"A pound a week? Are you joking?" she replied. "That is so depressing. It would take me six or seven months to lose what I need to lose. I can't wait that long to look better. I want to lose it now. I am ready now!"

"Well, you might want it now," I said, "but that does not make you ready now. I am telling you that if you lose it quickly, instead of as the result of a changed lifestyle, you will probably gain it back. You cannot sustain that kind of deprivation. It rarely works.

"But, let me ask you a few things. Could you take a brisk walk for thirty to forty-five minutes every day?" I asked.

"Sure," she said.

"Okay, could you make a five-minute call every day to an accountability partner?"

"Yes, that is not hard," she said.

"Could you cut back on the bad foods by some percentage?" I asked.

"Yeah, that is not too much to ask. I can do that," she went on.

I continued with a few more things that are always steps in a successful plan, showing Jessica that each had three characteristics in common: *small, simple, and good.*

Each of the steps we were talking about was a *small* thing that was *simple* to do, but each was also a *good* idea for improving life in general, even for people who are not trying to lose weight. And I knew that if Jessica took those little steps, she would keep the weight off this time, breaking the hopeless pattern of big crash losses and quick regains.

Jessica began to get excited as we talked. The picture of simple life changes that add up to good results was getting traction. She was picturing it. Then it happened. I saw the wind come out of her balloon.

"What?" I asked, seeing her face crash.

"I was getting into your plan and then I thought about something. Each week I would go weigh myself and see that I had lost only one pound. Or maybe two. That would seem so insignificant that I would just blow it off. That is so depressing!" She was near tears.

"And that is exactly what I meant earlier when I told you I did not believe that it was the dynamics of your relationship with Reese that played the greatest part in your difficulty in keeping it off. I think it was the 'Jessica All or Nothing' dynamic," I said.

"What is that?" she asked.

"That is the manner in which you think about something that you want and do not have: *you want all of it.* You want the thirty pounds gone—anything short of having it all off right now is depressing to you. Here is what happens in your head: you think of how you will look having lost only a pound. And you get depressed because it is not where you want to be. It is not the end goal. You compare where you are at that moment to the end goal of losing all of the weight, and because one pound is not all of it, it is nothing to you. So you get depressed and give up. Since it is not *all*, it is *nothing*.

"But, here is what you miss. Thirty pounds is a sum of a lot of one pounds. No successful person ever lost thirty without losing one. Then another one. Then another."

I told Jessica that the successful person does not think about whether or not she has lost thirty pounds; she thinks of each day, taking her walk. She thinks of calling her accountability partner, of cutting out a snack, of spending ten minutes journaling. She focuses only on the little steps that add up. She practices something called diligence. *She does not judge how she is doing by the goal. She judges by whether or not she is doing the small things.*

"I am concerned that until you begin to value the little steps and focus on them, not the big goal, you will always get discouraged and give up. Success will seem too slow to you. You will always see yourself as too fat. You will always feel that since the hundred dollars you save is not enough to retire on, you may as well go ahead and spend it, not realizing that if you saved that hundred, and then did it again and again for years, you would reach your goal. You look to see if whatever step is required will accomplish all of it, and if it will not, you do not value the step. And yet, *it is that very step that would get you there.* That is what I am worried about."

Wresting away Jessica's demand to have it all at once was a hard fight, but we did it. She began to value a little at a time. And as she did, she turned into a person who was not judging herself by the goal, but instead by whether or not she was working the steps along the way.

If the ant picks up a grain, the city will get built. But if the ant looks at the grain and says, "That is not a city! What a waste of time!" there will be no city in the end.

All-or-nothing thinking keeps people stuck in destructive ruts. It certainly is a part of the reason that people fail to join my déjà vu friends. All success is built and sustained just like a building is built, one brick at a time. But one brick seems too small and insignificant for all-or-nothing thinkers. They have to have it all, and one brick, one dollar, one pound, one new customer, is not enough for them.

But déjà vu people are different. They value the little increments, the tiny steps. Several years ago a friend of mine offered me an opportunity to buy into a business partnership. At the time I had my eye on some other investments that had bigger, more aggressive goals. This deal was slow and had a longer paydown in smaller increments. The thing that led me to invest in it, however, was my friend showing me where he was at that time in the deal. Having invested little by little, year after year, he had paid down the debt through his profits. By that time he was retired several times over, enjoying at a relatively young age the fruits of one brick at a time. I liked his result. He was also a déjà vu friend, so I decided to do what he did in this deal. Usually when you do what déjà vu people do, you do well.

Because the payoff in this deal built itself one step at a time, I have to admit that I was not too excited about it. As I made payments into the partnership year after year to pay tax liabilities and pay down debt, the benefits seemed to accumulate so slowly as to be hardly visible. But hey, this was my déjà vu friend's deal. So I trusted it by proxy. I looked at some documents the other day, and I was shocked! In two more years I will be done paying it down, and it will be paying me! My déjà vu friend was right. One grain at a time and an ant can build a city; one payment at a time and anyone can build a nest egg.

Many people have applied this principle to paying down their mortgages. If you have a home mortgage, talk to your loan officer and ask what happens if you put a little extra into each month's payment. If there is no prepayment penalty, you might be amazed at what a little more each time does in paying off your house.

Does your garage look like a mess, but the task is way too big to tackle and do all at once? Go in there ten minutes a day and throw something out, or put it in a give-away box, or rearrange it. Do that for three months. Do your closets need a redo? Same formula.

Is your savings account where the financial counselors tell you it should be? Put just a little away each paycheck. It does not have to be much, just something.

Are you out of shape? Start with ten minutes a day. Build up to fifteen minutes a day, then twenty, until you get to your goal.

Do You Want to Be a Novelist?

What if you have a full-time job, and you have always wanted to write a novel? Writing takes a lot of time, you tell yourself, so you give it up. It is an unrealistic dream for someone like you who has to work. Get real.

Well, that is exactly what John Grisham, one of the biggest-selling authors of modern times, did. He got *real,* meaning he practiced the real way that things get done: one step at a time. While working more than full time as an attorney, he had the dream of writing a novel. Though many people in that circumstance would let their dream die, Grisham went the way of the ant. He got up a little earlier each morning and wrote a little bit. Slowly, one page at a time, over a period of three years, *A Time to Kill* was completed. Since then he has sold tens of millions of books and is an incredible phenomenon of publishing history.

What did it? Talent? Of course talent was involved. But, so was the principle of one brick at a time. Not having a lot of resources or all the time in the world, he still did not settle for nothing. He wrote a few paragraphs each day. I do not know whether he observed the ant or not. I have no idea where he learned the method. I only know that if you write a little each day, before too long you have a book.

It was the method Tiger Woods used: one practice ball at a time. It was the way my business friend made hundreds of millions: one phone call at a time. It was also the way another friend who built a portfolio of clients did it: one deal at a time. Spend an hour at your flowerbed watching a rose. If the rose had the all-or-nothing attitude, it would cut itself down after the first week! Can you see it grow? No, you cannot, because the steps are too small to be seen. But give that flower a couple of weeks and see what happens. Growth too small even to notice blossoms into one of the most beautiful creations in the world.

It is the method used by anyone who has ever accomplished anything substantial, because that is the way the universe is designed. Things grow one little bit at a time, and it all adds up. Thus:

Wanting it all keeps you from having any.

---

9 Things You Simply Must Do

But I Want It *Now* . . .

Closely related to *I want it all* is its sister, *I want it now!* In my first book, *Changes that Heal,* I wrote that the shortcut is always the longest path. Often when people come to me with a problem, I will listen as they describe it and tell them that it can be resolved. There is hope. We know how to fix this.

"Great!" they say. "How long will it take?"

I will tell them the amount of time I think will be required, and that they need to commit to the process at some prescribed interval, say weekly. (You can see the pattern here: one week at a time, one grain at a time . . . ?) Many commit to the process, pick up their grains each week, and slowly you see a city of wellness being built. It is a wonderful thing to see, and I cannot tell you how much confidence I have in that process. It works. Because of that, I feel so much hope when someone commits to it.

But some do not build that city of wellness. Why? Because they cannot be helped? Because their problem is incurable? No. They do not build that city because they want to construct it in a way that is 100 percent opposed to the process by which growth and change take place: they want it *now.* When I tell them that what they want will come to them over time but that it will come from doing a little work one step at a time, these people say, *That is just too long. I can't wait that long.* Then I tell them that their chances of success are extremely low by any other method, but I will be glad to refer them to someone who does short-term work. They usually take me up on that offer. That is fine, for short-term therapy, retreats, and workshops have much value. I conduct them myself. But I know that for these particular people, short-term work is not going to resolve their problem.

What often happens, however, is they call me back after some period of time and acknowledge that short-term therapy was helpful but that they're still dealing with their problem. Now they're ready to undertake the kind of therapy we talked about before, where they come regularly for a longer period and go a little deeper.

That is good news, for then I have more hope for them. The bad news is that in the effort to skip the time involved, they have cost themselves more time. They have lost all the time that passed while they tried to take the shortcut. They could have been further along if they had not wanted the results so soon.

Wanting it now keeps you from having it.

Taking the long road, one tiny step at a time, will actually get you there faster because you will not lose time by trying shortcuts. People who *want it now* face frequent discouragement because of their many false starts. They think they can do a crash diet, for example. They lose weight only to gain it back. They think they can get rich quick, and go from scheme to scheme when all along they could have been building a solid business or career one brick at a time. All of the attempts fail, and those attempts use up and waste precious time. In the end, the want-it-now people end up back where they started over and over again. That is the great paradox of wanting things quickly. It causes you to miss getting them at all.

One of the best examples of this principle is seen in the experience of some lottery winners. Did you know that nearly one-third of lottery winners become bankrupt? Unbelievable? Maybe not when you understand the principle of one brick at a time. They did not build the ways to handle wealth—the life, the character, or the wisdom. Just like those who succeed temporarily on crash diets, they are the same person afterward, so they reproduce the problem that they had before. We see this principle operating in young people who inherit a lot of wealth. They usually lose it because they do not have the skills and character to keep it and make it grow. They walk in the same old ways, not the ways of the déjà vu person.

One brick at a time teaches us that we can have much more in life than we ever imagined. A small-town lawyer can become one of the most widely read authors on the planet. A minority athlete can become the world's greatest player in a sport where minorities have encountered barriers to success. The sky is the limit. But they all reached it the way of the ant. They did not have to have it in an all-or-nothing way. They were satisfied with one page at a time, one practice ball at a time. Nor did they have to have it right now. They realized that time was part of the equation. By obeying the natural growth order that God created, they got in step with the universe, one grain of sand at a time.

WHAT ARE YOUR ANT FARMS?

Life is what happens to us while we are making other plans. But too often we get overwhelmed, like Jessica, when the obstacles we see standing between us and our goals loom too enormous to tackle:

- I have never succeeded before, in spite of many attempts.

- The distance from where I am now to where I want to be seems too great.

- The goal is just too big.

- Things are too messed up to have any hope.

- I don't have the skills.

- I don't have the resources, like money or help.

- I don't have the time to accomplish it.

There are other perceived obstacles to success as well. But when we analyze each of them, we can see that they can be overcome, one brick at a time.

But that is not all of the good news of one brick at a time. The other aspect is that it does not just apply to specific tasks, like losing weight or paying off a mortgage. It applies to virtually every human endeavor. Here are some examples of how you can change your life and succeed in areas you never thought possible.

If your marriage is faltering, restore it one counseling session at a time, one act of kindness at a time, one example of not over-reacting at a time, one box of chocolates or bouquet of flowers at a time, one doing-something-unexpected-and-sacrificial at a time.

If your relationship with your difficult teenager is strained, build it one moment of connection at a time. Don't expect instant maturity and then giving up because three hours later he seems impossible again.

If you are in sales, build a portfolio of clients one call at a time. Do not expect instant success. Meet with one prospect at a time. Sell one policy or widget at a time. If you want to start a new company or grow the one you have, get one more customer at a time. Get an advanced degree one course at a time.

If you are out of shape, exercise as we have said for ten minutes a day for one week, then go to fifteen minutes, then on up from there.

If you are single and dating, do not expect instant romance or love to be the immediate prize or answer to your lack of fulfillment. Successful relationships and marriages are built one minute at a time. One act of communication at a time. One conflict resolution at a time. One act of sharing at a time. Instant romance is an oxymoron, and the rocket will come crashing down as fast as it took off.

If you are single and not dating, build your dating life one grain of sand at a time, in the same way we discussed in chapter six. Meet one person at a time. Increase your network one person at a time. Go out on one date at a time, even if you don't think that person is the end goal.

If you are anxious and fearful about something, take one little step toward it at a time. If you are shy and afraid of meeting too many new people but dissatisfied with the limited social life you have, take one little step of going to a function and just saying "hello" to one person. You can be quiet the rest of the evening; just take that one little step. Next time, speak to two people.

If you are depressed, get out of bed and do one small thing, like going to the park and walking. Or call a friend to do something different one night instead of staying passively at home. Take one small step of calling a psychologist and making an appointment. Take one small step of going to a support group. Then go again. Take one small step of journaling your thoughts and feelings for ten minutes a day and deciding to change one negative belief or thought.

If you have wanted to have a social gathering at your house but it just seems too big a thing to handle, have a little one instead, and choose a smaller menu. Serve hot dogs. It will be a first step toward building a pattern. You will be on your way.

After Christmas or a birthday, when you need to write your thank-you notes but you are the type that can never tackle that big pile, send one note each day. Do your Christmas shopping the same way. Buy one present a month and you will be way ahead at Christmas. Tackle the office clutter in the same way. Ten minutes a day for a month.

Save money just a little at a time. Forget about the balance. That will compound over time and you will be amazed. Do not even look at it. Just make the little deposits.

I could list a million more examples. I am sure you get the idea, though, that whether you are trying to lose weight, build a business, build a marriage, raise a child, overcome a pattern, resolve a depression, or build IBM, it is done the same way: one brick at a time. One grain of sand at a time. One conversation, one lunch, one act of sharing, one sacrifice, one meeting, one new person, and so on.

And as time goes on, you, just like my déjà vu friends, will succeed, and others will look at you and say, *I can't imagine how he or she did that! What an accomplishment!* You can just look at the ant and say, *Thanks!*

8

PRINCIPLE 6:
HATE WELL

Certain things, if not seen as lovely or detestable,
are not being correctly seen at all.

—C. S. Lewis

IT WAS A DÉJÀ VU MOMENT. I had a new partner in a venture that I was really excited about. He was well regarded for his accomplishments in business, leadership, and philanthropic causes. I was impressed with his business background, as he had bought and sold a company a few years before for more than half a billion dollars, making a huge profit in the process. He was smart, creative, and capable. I looked forward to learning much from seeing these attributes in action.

I noticed that this man was very principled in the process of buying into the partnership. I was impressed with his thoroughness. Three people told me that he had called them to check me out, since he and I had never known each other. I remember thinking that if everyone took such care before joining another person in a significant relationship, there would be fewer problems in life.

The déjà vu moment came when he requested a meeting as a

result of a problem we discovered shortly after he joined the partnership. Our accountant found a debt owed by the partnership that had not been disclosed in the purchase (a credit to another company). Since this kind of accounting event is not unusual, I didn't give it much thought. I assumed the meeting was just to resolve the issue of who owed whom and work out the numbers—business as usual.

As we sat down I could tell that my new partner was not happy. He was not overtly angry or raging or anything like that, but you could tell that this was not going to be a cheerful meeting.

"Let me tell you why I wanted to get all of you together," he began by saying. "I do not mind problems. Business is about solving problems, and I do not get upset about them. That is all a part of doing deals. But, I *hate* surprises. This new information was not disclosed to me in the purchase process, and now it comes out. If I had known of it earlier, it would not have mattered. It is just a problem to be solved. What I have a problem with is that now I am surprised by something I should have been told earlier. I do not want surprises," he said.

This was interesting for me to experience. First of all, I understood how my partner felt. I would have felt the same way. Second, I did not foresee tension over this late disclosure because I could tell that he was reasonable enough to understand that the debt was a surprise to me as well. In no way had I concealed anything from him.

I was having a bigger experience, though. *I absolutely loved how he handled the situation.* The thought went through my mind, *This is what successful people do. This is how they operate.* I thought at that moment of several other déjà vu people who worked in the very same way.

We've looked at ways successful people focus on their internal drive; tolerate no negative energy; make decisions in the present depending upon how they affect the future; take responsibility and take action; and make progress one step at a time. Now we look at the sixth of the Nine Things: the ability to hate well.

WHY WE HATE

One evening as I was doing a seminar I asked people in the audience to list what comes to mind when they thought of the word *hate*. The response I got was a list of bad things:

- You should not feel it.
- I do it too easily.
- I feel guilty for feeling it.
- It comes from fear.
- I feel uncomfortable with hate.
- I am afraid to show it.

Such answers were pretty much what I expected, and they are probably typical of those most of us have when we think of hate. Principle Six's concept of *hating well* seems like an oxymoron to most of us. We try to get over hatred because we have all seen the destruction that it causes. We usually think of hate as a problem to be solved.

In reality, though, hate is one of the most important aspects of being human. It is one of the most crucial ingredients of a good person's character. *What we hate* says a lot about who we are, what we value, what we care about. And *how we hate* says much about how we will succeed in love and life.

What We Hate Defines Us

First, let's consider why we say that what we hate is important. Basically, we are defined in part by what we love and what we hate. What we love says what we will invest in, go for, move towards, give time and resources to, and orient ourselves toward with the best parts of who we are. You can tell a lot about people by what they love. You think differently, for example, about someone who "loves his family" as opposed to someone who "loves to win at all costs." What he loves gives you a window into his soul, and you know what to expect from him.

Likewise, we can know a lot about people by what they hate. A person who hates hard work, for example, causes you to wonder. Or one who hates weakness would likely cause you to keep up your guard. Hate gives us a window into people's makeup in the same way that love does.

What would you think, for example, about a person who said that he hates the following things: arrogance, lying, innocent people being hurt, harmful schemes, evil practices, telling lies about others, and things that stir up dissension among people?

If a person said that he hated those things, and his life demonstrated the truth of his claims, wouldn't you be inclined to like that person? Even trust him? Wouldn't it be easy to depend on such a person?

You could depend on people who hate the items on the above

list because they would endeavor to be the opposite of all of those things in their dealings with you. They would stand up against those evils to protect you if others tried to inflict them on you. Such a person would make a good friend. A passage in Proverbs (6:16–19) uses these same objects of hatred to describe God himself. We get comfort in knowing that he hates the things on that list because we realize that he is loving, and also that he will stand against those things when they threaten us. When we hear *what someone hates,* it tells us a lot about who he or she is.

That is why I loved that moment with my new partner. When he said that he hates surprises, I learned a lot about him. I learned that he liked to deal with things in the open. I also learned that he would take active steps to put an end to the things he hates when they present themselves. My trust in him grew at that moment. I knew that when dealing with him I was always likely to get the whole picture because that is what he values. He hates anything less.

We are created with what psychologists call *valences* toward different things. That means we have emotional and attitudinal stances towards certain issues in life. As Webster puts it, a valence is "the degree of attractiveness an individual, activity, or object possesses as a behavioral goal." Hatred is a negative valence. The things we hate are those that are least attractive to us. That is why I trusted my partner. I found that he is not attracted to less than total disclosure and honesty. He would likely move away from deceit and shun being a part of it.

That is how our hates form who we are, at least in part. Our character is in some ways formed through a process of what we move against, or as psychologists put it, what we differentiate ourselves from. For example, if we hate duplicity, then we want to be different from duplicity. So we move toward being the opposite, which is a move toward being open and honest. Thus:

Character is in part formed by what we hate, because we move to be different from whatever that is.

OUR HATRED PROTECTS THE GOOD

So the first thing that hate does for us is to help us move against certain traits and issues, thus becoming different from them. Think of it as being like the energy that pushes a boat away from a dock. We use the energy of hate to move against that trait so that we are not docked to it. We push away from attaching ourselves to that thing we hate. That gives us a real separateness from that thing, so that we do not drag it with us across the sea. In that way we eliminate the danger of having it become a part of us, as we do not allow ourselves to become attached to it. Our hatred of it serves as a protective force.

You could see that protective force working in my business partner. He was in little danger of becoming a duplicitous person because he was diligently engaged in pushing away from surprises and secrecy. He was heading in a different direction, one of openness and light. Without a similar hatred of such things, many people are vulnerable to either being overcome by them or actually taking on those attributes for themselves.

The second way hate benefits us is that it causes us to protect what we value. We hate it when things we love are threatened, so we move to protect them. In that way, hate is a protective emotion, urging us to stand for good things. My friend was taking a stand for operating openly in the light. He was protecting what he loved— honesty and disclosure.

The third way that hate is a good thing is the flip side of protection. Hate moves to destroy bad things, which are often the things that threaten the good. The hate of evil protects the good not only by shielding it but also by cleansing the world of the bad things that move against it. When we hate the evil around us, we move to get rid of it as an act of love. As the apostle Paul wrote, "Love must be sincere. Hate what is evil; cling to what is good" (Romans 12:9).

Hate is part of the immune system of your soul. Your physical immune system is an amazing part of your body's makeup. Think of what it does. When a bacteria or virus invades your body, your immune system identifies it as harmful and moves against it immediately. It confronts the invader and puts up a marker to identify it and describe what it is like. Your immune system has a cell that tells the rest of your cells, "This is a bad bug. Kill it!" The evil cell is immediately surrounded, giving protection to good cells. Enemy neutralized. Crisis prevented.

That is what hate does. In the same way that your immune system hates infection, the hate within your character identifies things in your life as evil. My friend had an active immune response to bad business dealings. He immediately moved against them, destroyed the threat, and protected the good things in the business relationship. That is exactly what hate is supposed to do.

How We Hate

What we hate is important in defining who we are and what we stand for and against. But another important aspect of hate is *how we hate*. Déjà vu people hate in a certain way. They can be depended on to hate in a way that *solves problems* as opposed to *creating* them. That was one of the aspects that I loved about my partner. He did not storm into the meeting enraged and yelling about the issue. He did not put anyone down or say anything hurtful. He went after the issue in a constructive fashion and solved a problem in the process. That is one of the things that made me trust him more, as well as one that reminded me of other successful déjà vu people I had seen do the same thing.

Successful people move against the problem,
and show love and respect to the person at the same time.

Hating Unwisely

Some of the worst diseases are of the class called autoimmune. Within that classification are diseases in which the immune system starts attacking the body itself instead of the disease. The healthy cells and organs are attacked, and health is destroyed in the process. A system designed to protect the good and destroy the bad goes wrong and begins to do the opposite. It causes more harm than good.

The same thing happens when a person does not hate well. He uses his hatred in a way that hurts things he cares about, such as people, a home, or even himself. It can be an ugly autoimmune disease of the soul and life. That is why I said earlier that the "how" of hate is as important as the "what." Successful people tend to hate in a certain way, and that way does what a good immune system is supposed to do: it preserves life. Non-successful people often fail because their hatred is not serving them or the things that they care about. Instead, it is doing the opposite—attacking and destroying the very things that they care about.

Jodi found herself attracted to Tony right from the moment they met. He was spontaneous and creative. His ability to make her laugh seemed to set her free in ways that she had never known. She loved so much about him. As their relationship grew, it was as if she had found new air to breathe.

Soon after they were married, however, a pattern emerged. His creativity and spontaneity began to lose some of its luster as she experienced the other side of it, which was a lack of organization and structure. He was, for the most part, responsible and a hard worker. But he was not very organized about it and did not have a high need for things to be orderly. This sometimes showed up in the way he kept the finances and his schedule, and at times things slipped through the cracks.

When those slips affected Jodi, the relationship would not go well. Instead of seeing his lack of organization as a problem to be talked through and solved, she would get very angry. At times, she would erupt and call him names, saying he was irresponsible and a loser. Her value of his humor and spontaneity began to diminish, and her disdain for him began spreading over the landscape of their relationship. She began to get more and more negative. Her hatred of his disorganization was becoming an autoimmune response.

The more she criticized him, the more he withdrew and resisted

147

her. Occasionally he would get angry and react, but for the most part he just wanted to stay away from her, finding things to do late at the office, spending more time on the computer instead of interacting with her when he was home.

They were locked in a cycle. She overreacted to his not being all that she wanted him to be and came at him with anger and judgment. He detached from her and passively resisted doing things that she wanted him to do, thus making the cycle worse. That is when they finally came in for counseling.

When I asked what brought them in, Tony began. "I have let her down a lot," he said. "I sometimes don't do all the things around the house that I should be doing, and I disappoint her in other ways too. I realize that. So, I guess I need to understand how I can do better."

"Is that the way that you would describe the problem?" I asked Jodi.

"Sort of. But I think to call it 'disappoint' is kind of a lame cop-out," she said.

"What do you mean?" I asked.

"It's worse than 'disappoint,'" she explained. "He totally drops the ball, and our life is a joke. I can't depend on him for anything."

I felt my spirit sink. I had no idea as to the extent of Tony's lack of performance. But I did know contempt when I saw it, and no matter what he was doing, I knew that her disdain was going to be a big issue before they could get better. It was not so much in the actual words she said; it was in the expressions and tone in which the disdain came across. It was poisonous and ugly. I felt that she was the last person in the world anyone would want to do something nice for, and I had to fight myself to keep from immediately siding with Tony.

"Sounds like you have some strong views about him," I said. I could not muster saying the word feelings because she was not sharing feelings. She was way past them. Hers was a view, a stance, an attitude: of contempt. I had to see what that was about.

"Well, anyone would have strong views," she replied. "How would you feel if you went to a department store, tried to use your credit card, and found that it was at the limit because he forgot to pay the bill? How would you feel if you were always having to nag someone to get him to do the things he promised to do?"

"That would be frustrating and sad," I said. "But it seems that you feel more than frustration or sadness. Tell me about how you experience it."

"I hate it," she said. "I hate it. I can't stand to live this way. It is like he goes out of his way to make our life more complicated and hurt me. I don't understand how he can know what bothers me and still do it over and over. It is clear that he doesn't care what bothers me. I hate it and I can't stand it anymore. Is that clear enough for you?" She looked at me with disdain similar to that which I had seen directed at him.

"Very clear," I said.

I did not explain to Jodi exactly what I meant by "very clear." It was clear that she "hated it, and could not stand it anymore." I understood that. What was also clear, however, was *the way that she hated it,* and how it was so unlike the way that my déjà vu friends hated. The way that she hated his lack of performance was more problematic than his failures. She was having an autoimmune response. Instead of aiming her hatred at things worthy of hate (which his issues were not, as she had greatly exaggerated them) and using it to bring about health, her hatred was attacking and destroying the things that she loved and were good: her husband and her home. She was not doing much to be a redemptive force in dealing with the problems, and instead was causing more pain than she was resolving.

As I probed deeper, I found that her disdain for lack of performance was being communicated to their sons as well. They often suffered the same kind of attitude that she had toward Tony and she never apologized for her reactions because she did not see them as a problem. Although she was poisoning her relationship with her son, she so *hated* lack of performance that that was all she could see.

She was no easier on her own failures than the failures of others. When she disappointed her own internal standards, there was hell to pay with herself as well. The immune system of her soul was not working. The hate that was meant to take a stand against destructive things was taking a stand against the things most dear to her. Something that was designed to protect good things and destroy bad things was doing the opposite.

Think of my déjà vu friend in comparison. What if he hated surprises in the same way that Jodi hated them? What if he had come into that meeting and expressed disdain for me, the accountant, and the whole partnership? What if he had communicated with the same poisonous tone and judgmental attitude that Jodi had? What if he saw me as globally worthless as she did Tony? Where would we be today? Instead of being close friends and satisfied partners growing into new areas together, we might have found ourselves in the equivalent of a business marriage counselor's office with our attorneys, not being able to stand the misery anymore and battling out a way to end it.

In one instance hate was used well to solve a problem. In the other it was being used to ruin a marriage and a young family. How does hate become so destructive and get turned against things that ought to be protected? And what can we learn about how successful people hate well?

SUBJECTIVE VERSUS OBJECTIVE HATE

The difference between those who hate well and those who hate destructively lies in the difference between the two kinds of hate: subjective and objective. Subjective hate is like any other state of subjective feelings. It is a pool of feelings and attitudes that resides in our soul, waiting for expression. It is not directed at anything specific or caused on any given day by any specific object. It is already there, sort of like an infection of the soul. It just lives there.

But this subjective hate does not just lie dormant. It jumps out. It expresses itself if given the opportunity, usually when prodded by some incident that reminds the person of some significant hurt in the past.

If you have ever inadvertently cut someone off on the freeway and gotten a hateful, vengeful, or even dangerous response of road rage directed back at you, you understand. The appropriate response of the other driver should have been nothing more than a mild expression of irritation. Think about it. The other person was not hurt. He was not even made late. He did not have to miss getting to his destination. There was, in a real sense, no problem. Yet he responded to you like you deserved death and should be destroyed. Why?

Probably there was something symbolic in the incident that tapped into a pool of subjective hurt and anger that person feels. It aggravated a subjective stance that he has assumed in the world. If at some point in his life he had been hurt by being overpowered, for example, he might hate any situation that makes him feel powerless. Thus he has taken a very aggressive *valence* in the world to prevent that situation from ever happening again. When you cut him off, you made him realize his powerlessness for one second, and now he wants to run you down. His subjective hatred seeks expression.

Jodi was like that. She had grown up with an undependable set of alcoholic parents who always let her down. Her childhood was very chaotic and their non-performance had caused her great trauma as a developing child trying to make it day to day. She had never really dealt with what are called ACA (adult child of an alcoholic) issues in her life, and as a result those issues just sat there within her in highly subjective states of fear, hurt, and hatred for any kind of letdown by anyone she depended on. So minor disappointments by a husband or son evoked a torrent of road rage from her.

Unresolved hatred can cause all kinds of wrecks and destruction. Like autoimmune disease, it can be turned within and produce addictions, depression, anxiety, illness and disease, paranoia, lack of trust, confusion, inability to reach goals, and a host of other destructive results. Turned outward, it can destroy relationships and careers.

At other times, though, subjective hatred is not just about unresolved hurt from the past. Sometimes it is produced from a character problem in which a person's pride, or desire to control or dominate, produces strong feelings of hatred when thwarted. While many of these people do have unresolved hurt, they also have some significant character issues that should be addressed.

PRINCIPLE 6: HATE WELL

Subjective hatred blasts other people, causes overreactions, dissensions, inability to resolve conflict, broken relationships, and many other relational diseases. It has a life of its own, and it runs counter to the goals of those who carry it around. As a result, they cannot succeed in love or life because the subjective hatred is working against their best efforts to make good things happen. What is the answer?

Turning Subjective to Objective

The answer is to make the subjective hatred objective. *Transform it to the kind of hate that solves problems, protects things that you value, and stands against the things that you do not want in your life.*

To do this requires finding the real objects of the hate, making them specific, and using objective measures to enforce them productively, getting the rage out of the equation. This is what successful déjà vu people do. They can tell you specifically what they stand against, why they stand against it, and what they propose to do to solve the problem when those things occur. And they do it not with a hateful attitude but with one that is respectful, kind, yet firm.

Déjà vu people also add other objective measures to the process as well. Instead of walking around with subjective feelings of resentment and hatred, they pick an objective time and place to deal with the problem. They take it to the specific person with whom the issue is rather than dumping it on an unsuspecting driver in the lane next to them. They are very objective and specific about what the problem is, and the words that they use to address it reflect that same kind of objectivity in honing in on a solution.

Whereas Jodi would subjectively blow up virtually anytime and anywhere, a déjà vu person would choose the best time and place as well as a better procedure to solve the problem. Whereas Jodi might communicate emotionally charged, unsolvable accusations like, *You're always irresponsible and untrustworthy,* a déjà vu person would address the issue in exact terms, in a calmer tone, and present it as being solvable—something like, *We have a problem.* Tony's failures were not as much of a pattern as she described and were not worthy of the judgment that she dished out. But they were a problem, and a good immune response was called for. There was just no need for all the inflammation. A déjà vu person might say, "Yesterday, when I tried to use the credit card, it was over the limit because you did not pay the bill. This happened once before too. I don't like being caught off guard like that. Let's talk about how we can make sure that this does not happen again. I want us to solve this."

Subjective hate is global instead of specific. It usually comes down hard on the offender and does not separate the person from the offense. It launches bombs and hurts and destroys the individual as much as it deals with the issue. Objective hate takes a stand against the problem issue, but it also integrates with objective love for the offending person.

I have a déjà vu friend who puts it this way: *Go hard on the issue, and soft on the person.*

That is a good way of thinking about the difference between those who hate well and those who do not. Subjective hatred often loses the issue in the disdain and judgment of it all, and is very hard on the person. Objective hate is very laser-like in its precision when addressing what it is against, and very soft and intentional towards preserving the integrity and respect of the person, even if he or she is an offender.

One of the hallmarks of déjà vu people is that they tend to not escalate issues and conflicts; on the contrary, they bring order to chaos and resolution to difficult situations.

I was talking to a friend who was president of a large company about how he became successful, and he told me the following: "I am not really sure, except that I did learn one thing as a young executive. I learned that if I refused to allow the really difficult people above me to get to me, and instead found out how to solve the problems they faced, I always became valuable to them. It would always end up putting me in some path of promotion."

If he had walked around loaded with a lot of subjective hatred toward authority figures, he would have gone the way of many smart, gifted, and talented people who never make it. They feel like they just have to "put those people in their place," or some such nonsense, and lose their jobs or promotional opportunities in the process. They do not know the wisdom of Solomon: "A hot-tempered man stirs up dissension, but a patient man calms a quarrel" (Proverbs 15:18).

So to become a déjà vu person, you have to take the subjective hatred that you feel and make it objective. Figure out where it comes from. Put a name and a face to it. Put a time to it. If you have to go into therapy to do that, do it.

Jodi did it and she became a déjà vu person. She built a successful relationship with Tony and her children. But she had to make her subjective hatred objective. She had to realize that the pool of disdain she was carrying around was not caused solely by what was happening to her in the present. She had to look at the specifics of how her parents had let her down. She had to talk through those feelings, which were spawned by specific, objective incidents, in real time history. She named the times and the incidents. She put words to them. She finally named her alcoholic parents' behavior as the cause of her hurt and the object of her hatred. And she expressed the ways in which they had failed her. She forgave them for the things they had done, and she got healing for the ways they hurt her.

After working through all those feelings, Jodi could see specifically the values that were objectively important to her. She valued dependability, faithfulness, follow through, and trustworthiness. These were good things. But along with them she also valued love, people, the feelings of others, respect, and the like. When she put those objective values together, she had much more positive responses to people.

She might want to take a stand against serious infractions against trust or a lack of faithfulness, but she would want to do it in a way that preserved the other things that she cared about, such as the people involved. She would still hate a lack of dependability, but she would also hate hurting people who fail to be dependable. Expressing both of those two values together brought about a different response. She confronted more lovingly.

Jodi's new experience summarizes the two aspects of how déjà vu people hate well: it shows us *what they hate* and *how they hate.* In terms of the *what:*

Déjà vu people tend to have immune responses to things that are truly infections, poisons, toxins, and dangers.

Getting cut off on the freeway is not one of those. Mild lack of performance or imperfections by those we love are not among them. Small offenses do not require a declaration of war. In terms of the *how:*

Déjà vu people tend to address the real toxins of life in specific, effective ways that face the issues and respect the persons involved.

Assessing What You Hate

We saw earlier how what we hate in part defines who we are and what we are like. It defines what we can be expected to take a stand for. One of the most important principles is to keep the important things in life important, and to focus on what is vital rather than on those things that might not be as big a deal. This is often said in many ways, such as *Keep mindful of what is really important in life* or *Don't sweat the small stuff.* We have scores of colloquial ways of reminding ourselves that life has certain essentials that we do not want to compromise. And at the same time, we do well to not elevate small things to the same level as the important things.

This does not mean that we do not address even small, bothersome things that we do not like. In chapter four we saw the importance of addressing the negative things in life, no matter what they are. But not all these issues will fall into the category of things that we hate.

Neither does it mean that when we speak of hate we are just talking about anger and emotion. Negative emotions are of little value when it comes to solving problems. Our hate certainly has passionate roots and deep connections to the heart and spurs all sorts of feelings, but it is more than that. It is a stance *for* the most vital things in your life, and a stance *against* the things that would destroy them. It is a structure and a value.

Most of these vital things in our lives seem to be universal values. Few people would not embrace them. They tend to form the foundation of the way that we see life. Earlier in this chapter, I referred to a biblical passage that defines God by describing six things he hates. It shows how *hating well* displays exemplary character. Here is the scripture:

> *There are six things the LORD hates,*
> *seven that are detestable to him:*
> *haughty eyes,*
> *a lying tongue,*
> *hands that shed innocent blood,*
> *a heart that devises wicked schemes,*
> *feet that are quick to rush into evil,*
> *a false witness who pours out lies*
> *and a man who stirs up dissension among brothers.*
> —PROVERBS 6:16–19

The items on this list are not small things. Think of the times that you have seen people—or even yourself—victimized by the evils on this list. They cause pain and destroy people's lives. To hate these things is to take a stand against them wherever they appear, and to employ opposite attributes in our own dealings with people. That is the value of hating the right things.

Sometimes in a seminar I will ask the audience to think back to when they were eighteen, the point at which they became adults. Then I ask them to listen to the following psalm written by King

David and think about how their lives would have been different if they had taken a stand against the things mentioned here and not tolerated them:

> *I will set before my eyes no vile thing.*
> *The deeds of faithless men I hate;*
> *they will not cling to me.*
> *Men of perverse heart shall be far from me;*
> *I will have nothing to do with evil.*
> *Whoever slanders his neighbor in secret,*
> *him will I put to silence;*
> *whoever has haughty eyes and a proud heart,*
> *him will I not endure.*
> *My eyes will be on the faithful in the land,*
> *that they may dwell with me;*
> *he whose walk is blameless will minister to me.*
> *No one who practices deceit will dwell in my house;*
> *no one who speaks falsely will stand in my presence.*
> —PSALM 101:3–7

Think how different your life might be if you had lived out a paraphrase of this psalm:

"Whenever I see destructive behavior, I am going to leave that scene. I won't trust people who are betrayers so I won't be walking around with a lot of hurt. I will stay away from people who twist good things such as love or sex and use them in some impure way. I won't play that game. I don't want to be close to those who are slanderers and put others down. And those arrogant types who think they are so superior and try to put me down can just stay away. I want to be around good people with good hearts and spend my time with them. I want to receive what they have to offer. I won't be around liars and people who are not into truth."

How much better would life be if everyone adopted those values that David espoused, if everyone hated those evils so much that they would not participate in them. Non-participation is the ultimate hatred! There is no rage in those lines of David's—no screaming or ranting. He is just saying, *My immune system is not going to tolerate this stuff in my life. Period.* And when any of those evils did assail him, he would just activate an objective immune response that confronted the issue and stopped it from infecting him or his relationships. No ranting or raving needed; just a very clear stance.

So, what is on your list? What is worth hating? And where has hate gone awry for you? What do you hate that is really not "hate-worthy?" Where has subjective hate filled you up so much that it finds expression in ways and at times that are not good for you or for others?

YOU GET WHAT YOU TOLERATE

Just as water seeks the lowest level, dysfunction seeks the lowest level of tolerance. If your standard for what you require in life and relationships is low, bad things will ooze into your life just as water dribbles to the lowest spot of ground. If you allow mistreatment, then people who mistreat others will find you and you will get what you tolerate.

However, déjà vu people, you will notice, simply do not tolerate dysfunction. They hate it—wisely. They send out the antibodies, mark it for what it is, and end it. They do not destroy the person or the relationship in the process, but they do not tolerate the infection.

So choosing what you hate is serious business. What will you tolerate? What will you not? What will you work with and what will you absolutely under no conditions allow? Remember that what you do not hate well is going to find its way into your life.

Here are some tips that déjà vu people would offer:

Make Your Values Intentional

Spend some time thinking through your life to uncover situations you faced that were much like the evils that David shunned in his psalm, or like the seven things that God hates. Think about what you have found to be hurtful, and what you should see as worthy of taking a stand against in order to protect what you love. Make a list of your values. Pray over them. Ask the people who know you well and whom you see as déjà vu people what things in their lives are non-negotiable. Review the list periodically and see if you need to add anything or take anything away. Make sure that it includes all the basics that you should take a stand against, like dishonesty, abuse, disrespect, control, and oppression.

Build Up Your Immune System

Just like your physical immune system, your emotional and spiritual immune system can be either strong or weak. The stronger it is, the less we tend to get infected and the more we are able to be around sickness without getting sick ourselves. The weaker it is, the more we require supportive environments to keep us well. They need to be as germ-free as possible.

Assess how strong you are. You might find that until you get stronger, you should not be exposed to certain kinds of "germs" and "toxins." Certain people or situations may be too much for you. You would do well to find a safe place where other people can take a stand against hateworthy things for you while you work toward getting stronger.

Then take the necessary steps to strengthen your emotional and spiritual immune system. Find a support or recovery group. Get support or counseling if needed. Work out the toxins inside that are making you susceptible to so much infection. Deal with your dependencies on toxic people and other related issues. Do whatever it takes to get strong.

Deal with Your Subjective Hatred

Find the sources of your subjective hatred and, like we said above, make it objective. Put names and faces and times to the origins of your problematic feelings and attitudes. See if you have been subject to global feelings and assessments like Jodi was. If you have been hurt, for example, by a certain woman, do you hate all women? Or if by a man, do you hate all men? Make that anger and hurt objective to the one person who hurt you and do not generalize.

When you apply objective things like time, space, understanding, specific events, specific emotions, and specific places to the origins of your hate, you can begin to put them in their proper place. Realize that your hurt comes from a different time in the past, and let the span between then and now help you get a new perspective on it. Understand what the hurtful incident meant for you then, and what it has come to mean for you today. Think about what new understanding you can bring to those same kinds of events today that can reduce their power in your life. Work through the feelings and emotions of it all with a trusted person or group. When you trace the origins of your feelings to objective people or events, you can begin to understand them and sort them according to their value.

You must take from those experiences the things that you want to learn and make part of you, such as what kinds of people are untrustworthy and should be avoided, or specific skills that would make you stronger now and not susceptible to the same kind of injury again. Above all, seek healing and understanding for the parts of you that have been injured.

Mix Hate with Love and Respect

A déjà vu person shows up with what we call an *integrated* character. In other words, when he brings his hate, he also brings his love as well. His hate is integrated with his love and other values, such as respect for people, kindness, and forgiveness. That is how he can take a hard stand on a tough issue but remain loving and kind in the process. It is what makes him effective at doing confrontations, and why his relationships tend to move to higher levels as a result of confrontations instead of deteriorating into rage-filled messes.

You can take an absolute stand against something without being destructively angry. In fact, one's anger is often an indicator of how afraid he is of whatever he must encounter. As Proverbs 25:28 says, in essence, "An angry man is like a city without walls." In other words, when people do not have strong immune systems, fear takes over, causing them to get angry and lose control. Déjà vu people rarely lose control. They simply assert their stand against what they hate. They do it wisely. They do it well. And hating well always means lovingly, kindly, being soft on the person but very strong on the issue. By strong I simply mean not giving in. There is no need to be mean, loud, or ferocious. Strong means immovable.

So in your immune responses, show kindness. Just do not tolerate the thing that you have a no-tolerance rule against. Then your other values will also find their place as well—values such as helping the other person and restoring the relationship. If your immunities are strong enough, you can even be around the things that you hate without being infected by them while you are trying to restore or help someone. You are strong enough to "overlook an offense" (Proverbs 19:11). Everyone who ever helped an addict, for example, knows what that is like. Or anyone who ever parented a teenager.

Build Your Skills

Taking a stand against the things that destroy life can be tough if you have never learned the skills needed. Besides being strong enough inside, you might also need to learn some good conflict resolution or assertiveness skills. One thing that déjà vu friends always do well is resolve conflict, and that means being honest and assertive without losing control of oneself, getting manipulated, or freaking out. If you do not know how to do it, take an assertiveness workshop or a conflict resolution workshop. Get a book on the topic and do role plays with a friend. Watch others who are good at assertiveness.

PRINCIPLE 6: HATE WELL

Destructive or Constructive?

Whether you are going to hate is not an option. You have been created in the image of God to stand up for life and stand against things that destroy life. So when hurtful things happen, you are going to have a response. It is hardwired into you. Things that you do not like are going to happen, and you are going to experience negative feelings. The question is this: will that response be *constructive* or *destructive?*

You can respond in subjective, immature ways and destroy relationships, your career, and people you care about; or you can avoid responding at all and get yourself destroyed in the process, along with your talents, health, and many other things you value.

There is another way, the sixth of the Nine Things you simply must do. You can learn the way of déjà vu people, the pattern of hating well. That means that you will be one of those people who objectively choose what they will hate, and you will objectively decide how you will deal with those things when they present themselves. In the process, you will preserve most of the good things in your life, eliminate most of the destructive things, and experience much more success in both love and life.

9

PRINCIPLE 7: DON'T PLAY FAIR

The Christian ideal has not been tried and found wanting.
It has been found difficult; and left untried.

—G. K. CHESTERTON

OKAY, I HAVE A QUESTION FOR YOU," I said to the seminar crowd. "I sometimes give a talk entitled How to Destroy All of Your Relationships. In your opinion, what is the formula for destroying relationships? How do you do that? What are some ways that you have destroyed relationships?"

The answers started coming from the floor. Be mean. Lie. Cheat. Don't pay attention. Criticize, and so on. Of course, those were all good suggestions, and they would probably be pretty effective. But they did not anticipate the formula that I was about to give them.

"Here's all you have to do to ruin every relationship in your life: *Play fair.* If you play fair, you will ruin all of them. Some may go pretty quickly, others may take longer. But in the end, you will succeed. Play fair and all your relationships will be ruined."

The audience looked at me like I was crazy. And I understood that look, because the concept is counterintuitive. To play fair seems like such a good thing. We love people who play fair and dislike those who do not, right? Well, not exactly.

In this chapter, we will find that my déjà vu friends succeed in love and life because they do not just play fair at all. They know where fair gets them, and they want better than that.

Up to now we've looked at how successful people know that you must listen to your heart's desire; eliminate negative forces; choose the future by acting well in the present; take action and responsibility; take small steps to victory; and hate the right things in the right way. Now let's look at the seventh of the Nine Things you must do.

GOOD FOR GOOD, BAD FOR BAD?

The business deal that I was working on had taken substantial time and effort. There were several parties involved, and tons of work had been done to get the deal to where it was on this particular day. I had high hopes for success. Things looked good.

My meeting that day was supposed to be somewhat of a celebration. The man I was meeting with was the last pivotal person to make it all work. I had been getting to know him better, and at this point I had found him interesting, creative, and smart. So I had been looking forward to this day when we were to sign up to go the next step. Then it happened.

We were eating lunch and discussing all we had gone through to get things to that point, and how happy we were that it had all worked out. That is when he said, "I am looking forward to working with you. You seem like a trustworthy person who does good work. I am like that myself. You can depend on me; I will do my part. You do your part, and I will do mine. Do me right, and I will do you right. But, don't screw with me, or you won't like it. Mess with me, and I will mess with you right back. Treat me well and we'll be fine."

At that moment, I knew our deal was off. There was no way I was going forward with this man. Why? *He just wanted to play fair.* As long as I was treating him well, he would treat me well. Things would be fine. But if I gave him less than he desired, then he was going to do the same back at me. Good for good, bad for bad. That is only fair.

And it will destroy every relationship in life.

So I told the man that our deal would not work for me, and I would not be able to move forward.

Later when I was explaining my decision to some other people, I said that that kind of relationship will not work. I do not like to be in partnerships where the attitude is to give each other just what we deserve. That is certainly fair, but if I enter a relationship with you, I want *better* than fair from you. I do not want to fail and have you get back at me in some way to even up the score.

"I understand that principle to be fair," I explained, "but I want more than that. If I make a mistake, I want you to help me, not get back at me. If I fail, that is exactly when I need you to do better, not worse. If I do something wrong, I need for you to rise above it and show me, and be a force to get us on the right track, not to cause the situation to deteriorate into getting even."

I would want to do the same, I continued. If a person with whom I had a relationship made an error or did something detrimental to the relationship, I would want to help him or her see it, fix it, and do better. I would want to be a force to help raise them up, not drag them down. That is the only kind of partnership I want to be in.

The Philosophy of the Masses

My potential partner was not a bad person. He was one of the good guys. He did not go around looking for ways to hurt people, nor did he do them wrong to benefit himself. He was not a crook. He was honest. In short, he was like most of the people we run into on a daily basis. They are nice as long as they are being treated nicely. They are loving as long as they are being loved. That works well, for a while.

Marsha called our radio show with a question about her marriage.

"I need to know how long is long enough," she said. "How long do you put up with a problem and hope it is going to change, and when do you pull the plug and get on down the road?"

"You are talking about your husband?" I asked. "Are you wondering if you should divorce?"

"Yes, exactly. I don't think he is going to change," she said.

"How do you know that? What have you tried?" I asked.

"Well, we tried counseling, and all either of us did was go in there and tell the counselor how bad the other was. It was just a griping session about each other's faults. I got mad at him and he got mad at me. I have tried and tried, but no matter what I do, it is not enough. It is just not going anywhere, and I am tired of trying," she said. I could hear the agitated despair in her voice. She did not seem mean in her anger; she was just angry that she could not get the man she loved to come around, and she was staring hopelessness in the face.

"Are you the one who tries harder?" I asked.

"Yes, it seems that I am the one who is pushing to make it better," she said.

"So, can I assume that you are the more mature one in the relationship?" I asked.

"Yes, I think so," she said, a little reluctantly. "I am the one who pushes for our relationship to be better."

"Well, okay, let's assume that you are what you say you are. But if that is true, there is a problem. If you are the more relational one, the more mature one, then you are the one who has the greater responsibility. If you have more ability than he, then you have more responsibility to make it better," I said. "And the situation you have described is one in which you and he go into counseling sessions and each of you does the same thing. He blames you; you blame him. If this marriage is going to work, then you have got to do better than that. You have got to love him in a more mature way."

"What do you mean!" she asked, sounding a little ticked, as if I were suggesting that she just take whatever he dished out in the name of love. That is nearly always the fear of someone who is getting mistreated when you tell them to love better than they are loving presently. They think you are suggesting that they become a doormat with no boundaries, and just take it. That is not what I was saying at all.

"What I mean is that your 'maturity' and your 'love' is a dependent maturity and a dependent love. You depend on him to treat you well in order for you to treat him well. To make this better, you are going to have to rise above needing him to be mature and remain mature even when he is not," I said.

"I did that!" she retorted. "And it did not work."

"How did you do it?" I asked.

"Well, I decided that I was sick of the blame game, and I was going to stop blaming him and be nice to him to see if that would make things better. And it did. For about three months he responded. He was actually nicer. But in the long run, it didn't work."

"What happened?" I asked.

"We were in counseling, and we were getting better because I was treating him better. But then one day I made one little slip up and he blew up again. I made one tiny mistake, and he went right back to the way he was. That is what I mean. I tried and it did not work," she said.

"So what did you do then?" I asked.

"When?" she said.

"When he blew up at you. When he stopped responding to your being nice, what did you do?"

"Well, I got mad. I was furious because I had tried so hard for three months. And then I failed just one time, and he blasted me all over again," she said.

"But that is exactly what you did to him," I said.

"What do you mean?" she asked.

"As soon as he failed you one time, you let him have it back. So how are you any different? He was responding well to you for three months and you were happier. And then he blows up one time, and you throw it right back at him. So, how can you tell me that you are loving him in a more mature way than he is loving you? You do the same thing that he does: you love him as long as he is responding the way you want, and then the moment he does not—boom! You regress. Tit for tat.

"When you said that you had taken a more mature stance than he was taking and you were nice to him for three months, that really was not true. You were nice because he was responding well. But the moment he did not respond well, your 'mature love' was over and you were right back where you started. All it took was for him to make one little screw up."

She went silent for a moment. I could tell that she got it. "So what do I do?" she asked.

And that is the big question. What do we do when we get less than we deserve in a relationship? Or in a business deal? Or in life itself? *Fair* is giving good things to others as long as they give good things to us. Then if they fail us in some way, we respond "fairly." We give it right back to them, either at the moment or soon thereafter. Either our words or our actions say, *That's not fair. Therefore, I am not going to do good to you any more. In fact, I am going to give you exactly what you are giving me. Then you can see how it feels.*

The problem is that operating by the principle of playing fair, all it takes for any relationship to go sour is for one person not to perform, then the other one will do the same. There is an interlocking dependency: the other person must be good so I can be good. In this kind of dynamic, we need the other person to be loving in order for us to love them, or to behave maturely in order for us to behave maturely toward them. And no one ever performs perfectly, so that is why all it takes to drag a relationship down is one failure. Under the "play fair" system, deterioration is inevitable. See if these examples sound familiar:

- One person is a little withdrawn, so the other feels abandoned and gives the silent treatment.

- One person is a little sarcastic, so the other one is sarcastic back.

- One person gets a little angry, so the other one snaps back.

He Started It!

In each of these scenarios, what do you think the next step should be? Usually the one who began the cycle is not suddenly going to rise above it. More commonly he or she just hits the ball back over the net. The game is on, and there is no referee until the players get with the marriage counselor, to divorce court, or into legal arbitration to undo the business deal.

It's like the age-old interaction of two children on the playground when the parent says, "Don't hit your brother!"

"He hit me first!"

The one caught hitting feels that he did nothing wrong because his brother started it. In fact, that seems to be the mantra for kids who have not yet learned to interact maturely. . . . *He started it!* As if as long as I did not start it, I am innocent and justified in retaliating.

And when you think strictly in terms of fairness, that mantra really does hold true. We usually do not hold a person at fault who hits back in a fight that he or she did not start. The other person had it coming, we say. The truth is, that is right.

But the problem is that while *tit for tat* is fair and just, the end result is that the relationship is over, at least for the moment. It has broken down. And the vitriolic exchange that caused the breakup leaves things worse after the interchange than before it. No good thing has happened, and no positive change has occurred. Now there are two hurts instead of one. There is no resolution, just a smoldering need for revenge. Wrath and anger are vented, but nothing is gained, no problem is solved. The only ones who benefit are the attorneys.

The sad reality is that this is the philosophy of the masses. Good people, fair people, get divorced every day. Good and fair business partners split up every day. Good families get estranged every day. How often have you heard, *I can't believe they split up. They both are such good people; how could that have happened?* And it is true. They are both good. Fair is good. But fair does not work; so good people fail at relationships every day.

GETTING BEYOND JUST FAIR

So what do we do? When someone fails us, do we just act as if nothing happened? Do we take it and become doormats? Will that help a relationship? Certainly not. If there has been any breakthrough in recent decades, it is the popularization of the very helpful awareness that codependency and enabling are bad, destructive things. They are not the answer at all. They only make things worse. So what is the answer?

Here is Principle Seven expressed in three ways more eloquently than I could ever attempt:

If you love those who love you, what credit is that to you? Even 'sinners' love those who love them. And if you do good to those who are good to you, what credit is that to you? Even 'sinners' do that. And if you lend to those from whom you expect repayment, what credit is that to you? Even 'sinners' lend to 'sinners,' expecting to be repaid in full. But

love your enemies, do good to them, and lend to them with-
out expecting to get anything back.

—LUKE 6:32–35

Do not repay anyone evil for evil.
Be careful to do what is right in the eyes of everybody.
If it is possible, as far as it depends on you,
live at peace with everyone.

—ROMANS 12:17–18

Do not be overcome by evil,
but overcome evil with good.

—ROMANS 12:21

The answer is very simple, and very hard to do. It is the way of déjà vu people:

Give back better than you are given.

People who succeed in life do not go around settling scores. They do not even keep score. They "run up the score" by doing good to others, even when the others do not deserve it. They give them better than they are given. And as a result, they often bring the other person up to their level instead of being brought down to the level of the other. They are a redemptive force carrying a good infection wherever they go, infusing relationships with health; infusing businesses with health; and infusing communities with health. They change things for the better. They give back better than they are given.

Jesus' words in the first passage above simply describe the truth of what we saw earlier. Pretty much everyone loves those who love back. Most people do good to those who do good to them. My almost business partner did as much. Even banks give money to those who are going to repay. Big deal. When a relationship operates on the same principle, an inherent problem looms in the background. As soon as there is a late payment, the relationship goes into a negative dynamic.

But to do good to people who do not deserve it is an altogether different matter. It is the law of love. It has the power to improve those who are failing. It has the power to turn them around. Instead of lowering yourself to their level, you elevate them to yours. This is the only way that good relationships continue and the only way that problem relationships get better. Let's take a look at how déjà vu people make this principle work.

Get Rid of Anger

There are different ways of responding to anger. We'll look at two that are problematic and one that is better.

The first way to respond to your anger is to not feel it, to be out of touch with it, to deny it, and to not allow it to tell you that something is wrong. People who do not know that something is making them angry are out of touch with what they want and cannot solve problems. They let negative things continue, or they go dead inside, or they do something passive aggressive or unhelpful.

The other problem way of handling anger is to use it to get back at those who wrong you—to put them down, hurt them, lash out, shame them, or manipulate them into improving. Some people do not even think of their anger as a problem. They just let it fly, as a fair and just response to an offense. But such responses do not help because they put other people on the defensive. Their anger does nothing to reach the other's heart.

Successful people know this. They do not blast people with anger. They take a third route, which is using their anger to let the other person know that there is a problem. Then, they go and solve the problem by approaching the person in love, not anger, and facing the issue at hand. This is what we discussed in the last chapter, on hating wisely. Successful people make their anger objective, and its object is the problem, not the person. They are not doormats at all. But they fix problems in a way that treats the other person better than the other person treats them. In so doing they become allies with the person to solve the problem instead of enemies trying to win.

You just do not see people who are successful in the true sense of the word who are hotheads and have never gotten control of their anger. The successful ones do not let anger spoil relationships. They agree with Solomon: "It is to a man's honor to avoid strife, but every fool is quick to quarrel" (Proverbs 20:3).

Ask Yourself What Is Helpful

In spite of what I've said up to this point, the biggest objection that people have to giving good when they have received bad is their fear of becoming a doormat. They think such a response is bound to result in allowing people to "get away with murder." Nothing could be further than the truth. The power of the principle is that it will improve the relationship for both parties, not just for the offending one. I will explain.

The mature person in the relationship will ask, *How can I turn this around? How can I help? What does this person need? What could get him to a better place?* We said earlier that enabling is not helpful, and to give back something good is better than allowing one to get away with bad things.

It is true that sometimes one must set limits and impose consequences. That is playing better than fair. For example, if one partner in a marriage is being hurtful, perhaps abusing the other, abusing drugs or alcohol, or having an affair, it is not helpful just to take it. It would be more helpful to consider one of the following responses.

"I love you, and I want the best for you. I want you to face this problem and get over it. I will get help with you or do anything I can. But I won't allow this kind of hurt and destruction to continue with me. We cannot be together until you decide to do something about it. Let me know when you make that decision. Until then, I won't be living here."

"I love you and I want the best for us. But I can't talk to you without it turning into a fight. I want to be able to do that, but until we can do it, I want us to discuss the issue with a counselor present."

"It seems that this pattern of behavior we have talked about is not getting better. Can you see that? How can I help?"

Get Past Your Own Need

To make such a response requires that you get out of the basic dependent position that Marsha was in. Her "goodness" and "maturity" depended on her husband being good and mature. Such conditional goodness or maturity is hardly good or mature. Goodness and maturity are not dependent on another person; they simply *are*. To possess these attributes, you must practice them regardless of how you are being treated. That does not mean you are a pushover and allow destructive things to just go on without notice. But it does mean you face these things in a way that does not add another injury to the score.

The basic issue here is to avoid adding another hurt or infraction to one that has already occurred. To accomplish this, you not only have to get past your own hurt and need; you have to transcend it.

A friend said to me, "That all sounds good in theory, but I don't know how you can actually do it in a marriage when you have a real need for the spouse to be good, or trustworthy, or dependable, and he or she is not." Good point. It is difficult to do. But there is a principle here.

If it is true that your spouse is not being what you need, either for the moment or for a season, then that is reality. Your need is not being met from that source. To continue to depend on the spouse for that need when he or she is not going to deliver it, at least for the moment, is not wise. It is obviously not going to happen. It is like trying to get water from an empty bottle.

This is what my friend needed to see. Remaining in the dependent stance is what keeps you from being helpful to your spouse. Unmet needs create frustration, and you cannot be helpful to someone else when you need something from him or her. For example, when you need to be listened to, or cared about, or supported, that is when your friends, community, counselors, and support systems are vitally important. Do not simply go without having these needs met and be continually hurt, leaving yourself with no way of coping with the situation.

Thus, while working on the problem, you must find other ways and places to meet those needs. That means getting support to work out the relationship. That is how people turn tough relationships around. They turn to friends, or join a support group or a co-dependency group, to get their needs met so that they go into the difficult relationship from a full place instead of a needy and dependent place. When you are full, you can do what is needed in the difficult relationship to make it better. But if you are empty, you will just be sucked into the vacuum of immaturity that is being dealt to you in the relationship.

Successful people see life as a place to give, and as a by-product of giving, they receive back in the end. They are not giving just to get something back, but that is what happens. When a person takes the high road and helps a wayward spouse, sibling, partner, or friend mature through love and enforcing limits, they often get a mature spouse, sibling, partner, or friend in the end as the reward for their sacrifice. By "losing our life" as Jesus put it, we "gain it." But to demand it in the beginning, we lose it. The high road that leads to payoff is always the one that begins with sacrifice. That may not be fair, but it's true.

So, become responsible for getting what you need and maintaining your own emotional health so that the other person cannot drag you into the gutter. If you keep your feet solidly on the high road, you will be able to drag him or her up. It is like when the flight attendant tells you to first put on your own oxygen mask before helping a child put on hers. You cannot help another if you are deprived of the thing you need.

Sometimes Love Takes a Person to a Higher Level

Another friend tells the story of a time when his wife was out of town and he had to take care of their three small children by himself.

Being a psychologist, he was usually pretty good with them and understood their needs. On this particular morning, however, their little girl was pushing him past the limit.

He was trying to get them off to school, and she was lollygagging. He nagged her a few times but she did not pick up her pace. Slowly he began to get angry. He could hear her in her room, still playing and not getting ready at all. Her defiance was really irritating him.

He was on his way in there to let her have it when he stopped in his tracks. *If this were one of my clients, what would I do?* he asked himself. *I would find out what is causing this behavior.* He thought about it for a moment, and then he had it. He walked into his daughter's room, stooped down, and with his hands on her shoulders, looked her right in the eye.

She expected a scolding. But he said, "You miss your mommy, don't you?"

Instantly she fell into his arms and began sobbing. She could not even talk, so he did. "Yes, honey, I know," he said. "I miss her too. It is hard having her away."

After crying in his arms for a moment, she suddenly jumped back. "Daddy! It's late!" she exclaimed. "We have to get to school!"

His empathy had taken her to a higher level. Had he followed his first impulse and come down on his daughter, her behavior would have taken him down to her level of immaturity. He did not allow that to cause him to regress and act in an immature way. Instead, his love and softness melted her to a better place.

Solomon tells us that "A gentle answer turns away wrath, but a harsh word stirs up anger" (Proverbs 15:1). This wise father knew that principle, and it worked for him. But to make it work, he had to get past himself and his natural instinct to dish out what he was being given, even though his daughter "deserved" it.

Not giving others what they deserve is a big part of not playing fair. To give them better than they deserve is what the Bible calls *grace*. The word means unmerited favor. It describes how God treats us. Sometimes, as we said above, it means that we give someone loving limits and consequences if other things have not worked. But often, limits are not needed; only a little softness is.

Instead of blasting a coworker for not getting something done, the déjà vu manager goes in, closes the door, and asks, *Is everything okay? It looks like you might be getting a little overwhelmed or behind...*

Instead of riding a teenager for her non-performance, a déjà vu dad asks how things are going, or if it all seems too hard, or makes some other attempt to understand the teen before addressing the problem.

When a husband gets short-tempered or barks at her, instead of barking back, a déjà vu wife walks over and gives him a hug. *Little overwhelmed today, huh?* Barking is answered with kindness.

When those on the other side of a business deal do not do their job, the first déjà vu-type move is to ask how it's going, or if there is any way we can help from our side. *Seems like you guys might be getting overtaxed over there....* Often this kind of understanding is returned with gratitude and extra service. That is why good businesses give courtesy calls to those who are behind on bills instead of immediately turning them over to angry collection agencies. They know that the higher road is more effective in accomplishing their goal.

Ask How You Have Contributed

Few things loosen a gridlock in a relationship like asking the other person how you have hurt him or contributed to the problem. He is not expecting it. Jerri called in to one of our shows and told us all the ways in which her husband was angry and unloving to her. She painted a picture of a man who was highly reactive and pretty difficult to deal with. While I did not like the way that he apparently treated her, I wondered what it was like for him.

"Have you gone to him and asked how you make life hard for him?" I asked.

Silence. She did not say anything. "Jerri?" I said.

"Yes?" she answered.

"Are you still there?" I asked.

"Yes."

"What did you think about my question?" I said.

"I don't know what to say," she replied. "He is so difficult. Nothing I could have done could cause all his anger at me."

"I did not say it did. But you might want to try the higher ground here and give what you desire to receive. You want understanding, so why don't you first try to understand what it is like for him to be on the receiving end of your behavior. Ask what you do to upset him and how you can do differently. Ask what would help from your side."

It was an entirely new thought for her. Because he was the more difficult one, she had never thought about asking how she might be making things difficult for him. I did not blame her for his behavior at all. But I did think that by making the more mature move, she might win him over to maturity. If she made him feel understood, she might move him towards love. If that did not work, she could always fall back on the next step of setting limits. But we cannot require maturity from the other person until we are being mature from our side first. Going to him and showing that she cares how her behavior affects him is a step in that direction. *Overcome evil with good.*

Give the Opposite

Often we sabotage the possibility of getting what we want by giving exactly the opposite. It happens when we give just what we are given—when we are "playing fair." For example, let's assume there is someone you want to be close to, but that person disconnects and detaches. As a result, you withdraw your love. You pout or get mad. You withhold affection when he comes to you later. To give better would mean that you do not withdraw connection, but seek him. Instead of punishing, ask what is wrong. See if you are doing something that is driving him away. It solves nothing to return a lack of connection for a lack of connection.

If someone tries to control you, do not control back. Give freedom instead. Give choices. Speak to her control directly by making the choices that you want to make, and do not try to manipulate her or keep her happy. Then if she is not able to control you and gets angry, give her the same freedom that you have chosen: *I understand that my choice is frustrating to you. You can choose to be upset with me if you want. But this is what I need to do.* Live out freedom, and offer it to the other person.

If someone is perfectionistic or critical, do not criticize him for being critical. *I can't believe how critical you are,* is being just like him. Instead, accept him as he is, both the good and the bad, and empathize with the criticism. Do not agree with it; just accept it. *Seems like you are really frustrated that I am not meeting your expectations. Sorry that is so hard for you.* Such a response shows that you accept him even when he is acting like a jerk. You are not giving in, but neither are you returning criticism for criticism. You are giving the opposite: acceptance of where he is at the moment. Your response will likely disarm him, making him unable to pick a fight with you.

Remember, it is not a good thing to water a plant that you do not want or to fuel a fire that can burn you. Do not feed the bad, destructive things, but instead sow exactly the opposite. Do not let the other person get away with hurting you. That is not good either for you or him. But avoid sowing more bad behavior into the relationship. That is self-defeating.

What Goes Around Comes Around

Déjà vu people have transcended the need for revenge. Their first goal is to make things better for the other person or group. The other's benefit is their utmost concern. That does not mean they have no interest at all in their own benefit. It simply means that in their treatment of others, their goal is to do well by them *regardless of how they are treated.*

They are not interested in settling the score or getting even. Revenge is for immature people, and they know that ultimately the offending person is going to get what he deserves without his needing to bring it about. God and the universe have a way of making that happen, as does also the natural law of sowing and reaping. But even this ultimate payback is not something that déjà vu people wish on another person, and that is the true hallmark of their character. They truly want the best for others, even those who do not do well by them. Solomon expressed that kind of character in this way:

> *Do not gloat when your enemy falls;*
> *when he stumbles, do not let your heart rejoice,*
> *or the LORD will see and disapprove*
> *and turn his wrath away from him.*
> —PROVERBS 24:17–18

That is why déjà vu people are not full of bitterness and why others are not able to get them down. They do not let a dirty world stain them and turn them into "one of them." Instead, their goal is to turn the world and others into one of *them*—the kind of person who wants the best for everyone and wants everyone to do better than he or she is doing. And they're willing to pay a temporary price for that.

Because they are not looking for revenge, they often get the opposite. Good things happen as a result of their love and grace. People are transformed by their pardons. People are deeply affected that, when our déjà vu friends had them on the ropes, they did not knock them out. And that is just like the love of God. As the Bible says, he died for us "while we were yet enemies." He loved us when we did not love him. And as a result, God wins many people over to his side through such undeserved love. They become better people and pass that love on to others. That is how déjà vu people operate, and the fruit of that is more and more light and less and less darkness in marriages, families, workplaces, communities, and the rest of the world.

As for déjà vu persons themselves, what happens when it does not work out? They are not tied to doing just what is "fair." They are free to move on. They do not need to settle the score. They let it go and get on about their business. Because of that, they are not forever held up in the past, bitter, or dragged down by old hurts and grievances that are still alive in their souls. Forgiving and letting go have set them free.

10

PRINCIPLE 8:
BE HUMBLE

Pride is concerned with who is right.
Humility is concerned with what is right.

—Ezra Taft Benson

R YAN WAS AN ACCOMPLISHED PERSON who worked for a Fortune 500 company. Young and energetic, he had climbed the corporate ladder quickly. After doing well with a few assignments in Japan and Australia, he was a rising commodity in his field. There were several reasons for his success, but in talking to him one day I saw one of the main ones.

I had heard the story of how in a short amount of time he took an almost non-existent laundry soap business in China to one with sales of almost a billion dollars. It is an awesome accomplishment. Think about going into a country where you have never been, where you do not know the language, where you have no friends or support, and achieving such spectacular success. How do you do that?

I put that question to my friend. "What are the steps?" I asked.

"How did you make your business grow so spectacularly?" I did not expect the answer he gave, but after he explained it, I experienced another déjà vu moment.

"I got a job on a rice farm," he said.

"What?" I asked, a little confused.

"That is how I did it," he said.

"Excuse me," I said. "I was asking how you built the *laundry detergent* business into a billion-dollar enterprise. What does that have to do with rice?" I thought he had not really understood what I was asking.

"Well, I thought that if I went to work on a rice farm and worked with the people day to day, I would learn how they used their soap," he said. "Then I could begin to figure out what to do to build the business."

"What do you mean, 'use their soap?'" I asked. What could he possibly need to learn about using soap? He was already known as something of a soap expert who had built similar businesses in other countries. "Don't you just add water and use it?"

"Well, in each new country you always have new questions to ask about how they use the product, such as, do they carry it with them? How many times a day or week do they use it? Where do they store it? What size makes the best sense? Do they tell each other about it? Are they happy with it? I realized that I knew very little about how the Chinese used the product, so I figured that in order to sell it to them, I had better understand them first."

"But how did that help? Wasn't soap in China about the same as soap everywhere else? How did working with them result in the monster sales?" I asked.

"Here is how," he replied. "I learned that all the workers on the rice farms basically went to one spot to wash their clothes. They had to make a special trip from their homes to get to this certain place. It was a real hassle. For me the key was the reason *why* everyone made the inconvenient journey to this one spot. It turns out that the water in Chinese homes was very hard almost everywhere, but there were a few special places where they could go and find softer water. The softer water would cause the detergent to create more suds, which would result in better cleaning and use less soap as well. Their entire habits were dictated by the prevalence of hard water. It ruled their cleaning lives."

"So, how did that knowledge create sales for you?" I asked. "You could not solve the water problem."

"Actually I did," he said, "though I didn't change the water. What I did was take that information back into the research department and we developed a formula that made the detergent create just as many suds with hard water as it did with soft. So, for the first time, they could do their wash at home. It was a revolution of sorts. Then we created some ads that showed all those bubbles using the water within their homes, and we were off. Sales skyrocketed to $800 million," he said.

And that explains how the way to sell soap in China is to work on a rice farm. Or does it? Was working on a rice farm what did it? You could say it was, but that is not the real answer.

The real answer is the one to a more important question: *What was it that created the idea to work on a rice farm?* What caused my friend to do that? The answer: *humility.*

It was humility that made a billion dollars, not soap or rice. This simple but profound quality of déjà vu people, the eighth of the Nine Things, helps them succeed in both love and accomplishment.

We've seen that we must dig up and invest our talents, and move past the negative. We know we must make decisions based on their effects, and always ask how to improve a situation whether or not it's our responsibility. We achieve our goals through small steps, and protect the good with a healthy hatred. Now for Principle Eight and its enormous implications.

THE NEED TO BE GREATER THAN WE ARE

What does humility have to do with Ryan's story? We will understand the answer to that question after we first explore why the connection of humility to any real success is not always so obvious. Often we miss the ways that humility contributes to success in work and relationships.

Part of the reason for this is that our thinking is sometimes a little fuzzy about what it means to be humble. Have you ever thought about how to define humility? What comes to mind? Self-effacing, not taking credit, shying away from attention, nonassuming, and other terms are often used. There is truth to all of them.

Webster gives these definitions for the word *humble:* 1 : not proud or haughty : not arrogant or assertive; 2 : reflecting, expressing, or offered in a spirit of deference or submission (a *humble* apology); 3 a : ranking low in a hierarchy or scale : INSIGNIFICANT, UNPRETEN- TIOUS; b : not costly or luxurious (a *humble* contraption).

Through these definitions and others we can get a general feel for what it means to be humble, as opposed to proud. And most people can "smell" true humility as well as the stench of arrogance or pride that is its opposite. We know it when we see it.

But how do we understand humility in ways that we can put

into practice? Ways that bring about fruit in our lives? How does the successful déjà vu person show humility? Certainly through not being haughty or arrogant, as the definition affirms. To defer to others is a sign of humility, and to assume a low ranking instead of having to be on top are all-important indicators, as we shall see.

There are other ways of demonstrating Principle Eight as well, and in this chapter we shall look at those and see how they affect the déjà vu person's ability to do well in life—even to sell soap. But one simple, guiding principle that encompasses many of the others is this:

Humility is not having a need to be more than you are.

When I think of how the déjà vu person performs in the arena of humility, that is a pretty good description—to just be who he or she really is, a human being like everyone else, avoiding the need to be more than that.

It was that quality that sold soap in China. It was humility that led my friend to get a job on a rice farm. He avoided the pride and arrogance that others might have exhibited, thinking they already knew how to sell laundry soap in China. It would have been easy for him to assume that position, especially since he had been so successful elsewhere. He could have thought that there was nothing more he needed to learn. His mantra could have been, *Get out of the way. Here I come.* But instead, Ryan assumed that he did not know it all, and like other humans, had something to learn in each new situation.

Driven by his humility, he did not make himself out to be "more than he was." Nor did he have to appear that way to others. The truth was that he did not know a lot about China, so he let that truth be who he was. Pride would have assumed or acted like he did know, but not the humility that allows a déjà vu person to be what he really is in such a situation: *ignorant.* That was the truth, and owning it gave him the edge over the other companies who *thought* they knew but did not.

See the difference? The competition did not know how to sell soap in China either. Ryan and the other guys actually were on even ground there. No one had an advantage. The difference was that humility caused Ryan to see that he did not know; pride caused his competitors to assume they knew more than they did. Humility always wins. It is the winner's advantage.

Think of people you have worked with who came into the company with a know-it-all attitude. Are they still there? Often not. Were they liked? Probably not. What was it like to talk to them? Did you feel listened to? Understood? Valued? Probably not. Did you want to go to the mat and sacrifice for them? Hardly. The arrogant ones who think they know before they know are always tough to deal with. And though they might appear successful for a short time, they ultimately fail to be successful because they never learn what they do not know, and they fail at relationships because they never learn that people do not like them before it is too late.

Just as humility sells soap, it can also build success in all areas of your life. Let's look at some of the important ways that humility contributes to success, and how lacking it can guarantee failure.

HUMILITY IDENTIFIES WITH OTHERS

It was a moment I will never forget. I was in the midst of one of the most difficult trials of my business life. I had hired a person to manage a company I owned which had a lot of promise, great assets, and many things that pointed toward success. I had a substantial investment in it, and thus a lot at risk. The person I hired was competent, I thought, and able to make it work.

For several months I had been getting very good reports from him. The returns were going to be excellent, and I was optimistic about the future. But then it all broke loose. A crisis revealed that the forecasts I had been getting were nowhere close to the whole picture. Not only would we fail to get the returns that were promised, we were in substantial financial trouble with payables and debt my manager had accrued far beyond anything I had been told.

He had misled me about the past few months, but that was not the worst of it: the future looked bleak as well. Most of the future business that he had claimed to have under contract was not a reality, and in fact, we had very little booked at all. At the same time, he had increased overhead by many multiples, and cash was draining like water though a sieve. I had no clue as to what I was going to do.

At that moment I got the last call I would have wanted, but the one I needed most. I was on my patio praying about the crisis and asking God for guidance when one of my business mentors and heroes in life called. He was a true déjà vu person. He had amassed many successes in his business career, accomplishing outstanding feats in his fields.

So here I was in the midst of my own failure, getting a call from someone I saw as always succeeding. As a result, I was a little embarrassed for him to know about the mess I had allowed myself to get into. I remember wishing that one of my less successful friends had called at that moment instead of one of my highest-achieving ones! But here he was.

He asked me how things were going, and I told him the whole sad story. I did not hold back any of the gory details, even though being real and authentic at that moment was hard. Such openness was a value we enjoyed in our friendship: total honesty and full disclosure. I told him the whole thing, how bad it was, how out of touch I had been with how things actually were, and how I had absolutely no clue about what I was going to do.

When I finished, there was a long silence. He did not say anything, and I pictured him on the other end thinking, *What an idiot. I can't believe I have given time and guidance to this guy. What a waste!* I was waiting for him to say something like, "Well, Einstein, you created this mess, now I guess you have to live with it. But it was pretty stupid to let it get to this point without being more on top of it."

But that is not what he finally said. What he did say totally changed the whole picture for me and played a big part in my being able to turn the situation around.

"Well," he began, *"we've all been there."*

What? What did he say? Who is "we"? Certainly he has never done anything this stupid. What was he talking about? "What do you mean?" I asked.

"Just that," he replied. "We, including myself, have all been where you are. Anyone who builds something gets duped or fooled or surprised, at least once. It happens. And none of us ever sails through without losses and having things go really bad. By 'we' I mean any of us who try to step out and do things in business. We have all had this experience where we do not know the next step or how to get out of it. But you'll figure it out. I am confident of that," he explained. "In fact, this is when you are at your best."

PRINCIPLE 8: BE HUMBLE

At that moment something changed inside me. I knew that I was going to turn this thing around and make it work. I was no smarter after that phone call, and I had no more answers than before. But knowing that *this is a part of the path of success, and that even very successful people go through loss, failure, and crises,* gave me courage and hope that I had not had before.

God had answered my prayer for guidance in a way that I never would have foreseen by giving me a moment with a déjà vu friend who showed me that loss and failure are just parts of the path. I was not as stupid as I thought I was, and my crisis was merely a problem to be solved. I could do that. I did not know how, but here is the point: as long as I knew that my failures and losses, my mistakes and missteps, did not mean that I was an incompetent idiot, I could learn from them, unite them with my strengths, and make it all work out.

And that was the way of this déjà vu person. His humility was demonstrated in this fact: even though he was enormously successful, *he accepted his own failures and mistakes, and even saw them as part of the process itself.* He saw those occurrences as natural. "We've all been there," he said. No exceptions, including himself and even those who are more successful. This is an important quality of déjà vu people: they are not surprised that they make mistakes, and as a result, they can identify with others who do, give to them, and not judge them or wrongly judge themselves.

Identifying with other normal humans who fail leads to a number of success patterns, as we shall continue to see. The first two of these are huge factors in achieving success:

1. Successful people show kindness, understanding, and help to others who fail.

2. Successful people are not derailed by their own failures; they accept them as a normal part of the process.

The first certainly is an incredible gift to others. Over and over I have seen how déjà vu people extend themselves to serve others. They always tend to be givers of themselves. Truly successful people are givers, period. Success and giving are synonyms in many ways. Non-givers end up losing their success, or it caves in on itself as they inadvertently remove themselves from the larger picture of humanity. Self-serving success always implodes. Self-centered lives always create self-destructing black holes. Always.

But beyond the obvious gift that humble givers are to others, they also develop a lot of relational equity over time. They have extended themselves to understand and reach out to others, and as a result they are highly appreciated and loved. They create true networks of care in their lives. They experience high quality relationships as a result of their high quality of giving and understanding. People appreciate them, and their lives are full of love, both in the workplace and personally. The people they have identified with and helped are grateful.

And like everything else good and lasting, their giving is pure. It is pure because they do not give to get love or appreciation. They give freely because they truly do identify with others. And because they give freely, not to get anything in return, they are truly appreciated and *do* get a lot in return. People do not want to repay kindness that demands repayment, since it is not really kindness at all. But déjà vu people give themselves, expecting nothing in return, and for that they receive a lot.

The big result is that they are deeply loved and never alone in the world. And there is no higher success than that—to have deep, quality friends over time, friends that you are there for and who are there for you. This *is* success, and it also leads to other success, as you will always need the support of other people to accomplish whatever you do in life.

The second point mentioned earlier is huge for success as well. *People who win in life do not condemn themselves for failure; they accept it.* They learn from it. Failure motivates them to do better. They do not beat themselves up for it, and they do not begin to believe that they cannot accomplish something just because they failed. Because they are humble and identify with the human race that makes mistakes and fails, they see failure as normal. They expect it to come, so they are not surprised when it does. They use it and do not feel disqualified because of it. It is a paradox of monumental proportions.

Self-confidence does not come from seeing oneself as strong, without flaws or above making mistakes. Self-confidence and belief in yourself comes from accepting flaws and mistakes and realizing that you can go forward and grow past them, and that you can learn from them. You realize that your failure of the moment does not mean anything in terms of your ability to finally "make it."

So, the déjà vu person is not above the rest of the human race. He or she is firmly identified with it. The roots of the word *humility* itself tells us something about these people. It comes from the root word *humus,* meaning "earth," and also from a Greek word that means "on the ground." The humble person has his feet on solid ground, not in la-la land. He is firmly planted in reality, and that reality includes his knowledge that he is a down-to-earth, gifted, but imperfect person just like everyone else. It is not lonely at the top if the top is on the bottom. There is a lot of good company to be had there—like the rest of the human race. The successful person has no need to be more than who he truly is. That is humility.

The Biggest Sickness of All

I was once a consultant for the leadership team of a high-tech company which was in the process of selecting a new president. The founder had retired and it was time to find the successor. The search firm had narrowed the field down to a few candidates, and one in particular was the favorite of the founder and most of the board of directors. A meeting was set up in which the board, the founder, and the consultants would all interview him together.

We asked him a series of questions about such things as his vision, his plan for growth, his leadership style, how he would handle the markets. We also asked him about his former company, his performance there, why he had left, and other things related to his history. As he answered, I noticed a pattern, which began to give me a negative feeling.

The pattern was that everything he said seemed to place himself in a favorable light, sometimes even by putting others in a not so favorable light. He was looking better and better as he talked about himself and his performance. It was all good.

The feeling that I was getting slimed in some way began to grow. He was just so slick that I felt like I was in a room full of grease. It was a yucky feeling, and at the same time, a hollow feeling. It did not have that sense of fullness that one feels in the presence of a real person. I felt like I was listening to a snake-oil salesman.

He was nice enough—very gracious and not saying anything offensive. Why was I getting such a negative impression? Then I put the two factors together. The image he was painting of being without flaws and my own feeling of being slimed do indeed go together. That image is always a lie. We were being lied to in a very nice way. So I decided that I would give him an opportunity to correct my negative impression.

"I have a question," I said.

"Sure," he responded, smiling. I could feel his perfect answer coming.

"What were the biggest mistakes you made in the last company you led, and what are your biggest weaknesses? How do you think those weaknesses will affect the work here in this company, and how will you deal with them?"

The silence was deafening. No response. He just looked at me. He did not even look around the room. Then he said, "Well, I don't really remember any big mistakes that I made. The performance of the company, the stock price, all of it added up to a pretty good picture. I think things were really a big win there."

"Okay," I said, "I've seen the numbers. But what about you personally? How would you describe your greatest weaknesses and how they would affect us? And what would you be doing about them?"

Again he was silent for a moment, but then he spoke. "Actually, as I think about it, my greatest weakness is that I tend to push for the goal pretty hard, and come up with more visions and plans than some of the team members can keep up with. I run ahead of them a little too often."

I felt slimed one more time. I had asked for a weakness, and he had told me how creative, visionary, and strong he was. Too strong for others. I had to respond. "So your greatest weakness is that your strengths are so good?"

He seemed relieved that I had finally understood. "Yes," he said. "That is it. I go at such a fast pace that sometimes I can leave others behind."

"So that is your weakness," I said. "A strength."

"Yep," he said. "That is the big one."

The board finished with a few other questions and then excused him from the room. Several began to speak. "Great! Let's hire him." "Awesome!" "Really impressive. He is exactly what this company needs." "Very strong leader."

Finally I could not remain silent any longer. "I understand that you all really like him. But let me tell you something. This is a guy who thinks he is pretty much flawless and wants others to think that as well. He does not even know his own weaknesses. He thinks he has never failed. And I do not want him to learn about failure here, not as the CEO. This is a big job, and you want someone who has already done some failing before they get here. His fall is not going to be pretty when it occurs, *because he doesn't know how to deal with failure. He thinks he is above it,*" I said. "Get me a smart guy who is also smart enough to know where he is not so smart. If you hire this candidate, you are taking a huge risk."

People who think they have it all together are infected with a terrible sickness, and they do not even know it. They flatter themselves, as David said, too much to see where they miss the mark (Psalm 36:2). They are not wise in other areas either, because their wish to be seen as perfect and without flaw keeps them from seeing other realities outside themselves as well. Our CEO candidate was not being real, and that kind of denial and belief that one is all good is the worst sickness of all. "Do not do it; you will be sorry," I urged the board. "And put me on record as standing by that."

The company leaders did not like what I said and went on to hire him, with substantial stock options and other perks to get his greatness into the camp. A year and a half later they were buying their own stock back and trying to dig themselves out of the mess that he had created. He had deceived them by painting a better picture of the company than was real, and one that he actually probably believed. I do not think he lied, but he was out of touch with important realities because of his own overestimation of himself. In the end, both he and the company paid the price for his lack of humility. He paid by having his failure exposed, and the company paid by going through a takeover by a smarter group. Ugh. Big price to pay for wanting to believe in prideful perfection.

Déjà vu people know their weaknesses. They know where they are not good. They see where they have done it wrong, and they admit those things. They do not have the sickness of trying to "preserve the good self," as psychologists sometimes put it. They do not try to preserve a view that they are all good, either in their own minds or in the eyes of others, because they do not have such a view. Nor do they desire that others have that view of them.

Regarding their imperfections, these people do at least two things very well that build success, foster good relationships, and encourage learning, growth, and wisdom:

1. They admit it quickly when they are wrong.

2. They receive correction and confrontation from others well.

The first quality aids in learning and is always correlated with wisdom. We cannot grow and learn if we cannot admit our mistakes. How can we get better if we do not think anything is wrong?

To see our own faults is a key to growing in wisdom and learning how to make things work.

Closely related to admitting our own mistakes is responding constructively when the news of our imperfections comes from others. The way of the déjà vu person is to receive correction as a gift, and not to be defensive. Once when I was leading a retreat of leaders, an executive named Adam had just outlined his current situation to the others in the group. Then one of them asked him, "Would you like some feedback?" We could all tell from his expression that what he had to say would not be complimentary. He had seen something in Adam's life that needed some input or correction.

Adam's response was outstanding: "Of course, *give me a gift.*" Though he did not know the exact nature of what was coming, he was pretty sure that it was going to be some sort of criticism, though given in a positive spirit. He welcomed it. He saw that getting corrected or having his faults pointed out by someone wise was a gift indeed.

That is a consistent mark of wise déjà vu people. They are not defensive to feedback. Defensiveness is the mark of a fool, as you certainly know by experience if you have ever given feedback to a defensive person. It is a maddening experience. Here is how Solomon saw it:

> *Whoever corrects a mocker invites insult;*
> *whoever rebukes a wicked man incurs abuse.*
>
> —Proverbs 9:7

> *A mocker resents correction;*
> *he will not consult the wise.*
>
> —Proverbs 15:12

What a disheartening experience to endure in any kind of relationship! You give valuable feedback, and as a result you get insulted. Something that should be received gratefully is seen instead as a negative, and you get punished for offering it. You reap a storm of resentfulness for just being honest.

Such a prideful spirit that resists correction makes for bad relationships. And past that, it makes for a lack of success in the life of the defensive person. He is unable to grow and get past failure because he is closed off to the information that would help him.

Melissa experienced this kind of response with Tom. She loved him, but he would not listen to her feedback about how some of his behavior affected her. When she tried to tell him, he would get angry and feel victimized by the feedback. He could not see what was staring him in the face—a wife who genuinely wanted to be closer to him. His refusal to listen to her was getting in the way.

I saw this couple together and asked Melissa to tell Tom what was wrong in their relationship. She said, "Tom, I love you and I want us to be close. But when I ask you to help me with the kids at night, and you get angry at me, it hurts. It makes me feel alone. And then later when you want sex, I do not feel close to you at that moment. I try to talk, but you won't listen."

"See what she does?" Tom said to me in exasperation. "She is on my case about everything. It doesn't matter what I do, she always wants me to do something different!"

"I don't hear that, Tom," I said. "I hear her telling you how to get close to her."

"I try to get close to her," he said, "but she always finds something wrong."

"No I don't!" she cried. "I just need for you to understand what it is like with the kids all day and that I need some help. I need for you to share the parenting role with me when you are home."

"So you're saying I'm a lousy parent?" he responded. "See, Dr. Cloud, that is what I was just telling you. She is always saying that I can't do anything right!"

I wanted to try to clear up the problem and get him to hear, because it would change their lives. And eventually I would. But at the moment, all I could do was sigh. It was depressing. No, *he* was depressing. Unlike a déjà vu person, he could not take feedback. He resented it. He fought to hold on to the "good self," which made him unable to hear from her what he needed to learn in order to restore their relationship. If ever he were going to succeed, he would have to learn a new response to constructive criticism. He would have to stop feeling victimized when someone gave him feedback or correction.

Closely related is another kind of defensiveness in which some people are offended when they are questioned or critiqued. Once I worked with a man who was a good person, effective at his job, but had a lot of relational discord in his life. When discussing the people he was having difficulty with, he always seemed to talk about their shortcomings and how they were failing in the relationship. He said little or nothing about what he was doing wrong or what he could do better. He painted a picture of himself as a victim of the unfair or unloving people in his life, both on the job and in his personal life.

One day some things surfaced and I found out he had been less than straightforward with me. He had not overtly lied, but he had purposefully allowed a particular deception to go on that was hurtful to me. Valuing our working relationship, I went and told him that I felt a little deceived by what he had done. I was hoping that he could see the problem and understand it from my perspective so that it would not happen again. That is not the response I got.

"I have to tell you I really take offense that you would feel that way!" he bristled.

"Excuse me?" I said.

"I am insulted and offended that you would even hint that I have done anything deceitful," he said.

"Well, I am sorry that you feel offended," I said. "Why would *you* be offended by something that hurt *me*? The injury here is on my side." He had somehow managed to blind himself to the fact that he was the offending party, and had suddenly assumed the role of the victim instead of the offender. That is a common paradox with those who will not accept feedback. They hurt others and then feel like they are the injured party.

"I find it extremely offensive that you would feel that way," he said. Then he went on to tell me how right and just he was, and that I had no business feeling the way I did.

I walked away sad. I knew that deeper trust between us was not possible, as he was not willing to even consider how his behavior had left me feeling deceived. He was immediately invested in "preserving the good self," and not invested in how his behavior had affected me or our relationship. It was sad.

Then I thought about all the people that he had griped about in other relationships and wondered if they had behaved as badly as he had described. Had he ignored his own culpability in all of those situations as well? Seems possible. I felt for him, because until he could give up his defensiveness and his investment in being "good," there was not a lot of hope for deep and true success in his life. He was always going to hit a ceiling until he figured that out.

Later I had another meeting with a woman who had also done something that I felt could have been handled better. (It was a bad day!) I told her my perception of what she did and explained why it was troublesome to me. I said that I wanted to be able to trust her, but what she had done was getting in the way. Her response was that of a déjà vu person.

"Oh, my . . . I am so sorry. I can see that now," she said. "I did not realize how what I did would hurt you. I never want to do anything to undermine your trust in me. Please forgive me. Tell me more about how my action appeared to you and how it affected you."

I could feel the relational barriers coming down and trust coming back. She was truly more concerned about the effect on our working relationship than about being "right" or looking like she was "good." As a result, she became both right and good in my eyes. I knew that we would work it out. We discussed the matter frankly and sensitively, each coming to understand the perspective of the other. She understood my feelings and resolved that such an incident would never happen again. I totally trust that we will do fine from here on.

I reflected later on the difference between the two people. She was a déjà vu person, and he had a long way to go. Both situations resulted in a similar confrontation, and one relationship hit a wall at that juncture in terms of future trust. I will not trust that man deeply again until I see some change.

But with the woman, I have no qualms about trusting her in the future. The key to my trust is not in the fact that she made a mistake. Both of these people made mistakes. In one, the mistake put an abrupt end to our going forward together. In the other, it became a launching pad to going forward because of the way she handled the resulting conflict.

That is the key to what successful people do. It is not that they never fail, but rather in the way they handle their failure and imperfections. Instead of feeling compelled to be seen as "right" or "good," they are interested in what is best, no matter who is right or wrong. You never hear words such as *How dare you question me!* You hear *Oh, gosh. That's not good. Tell me more about how it felt to you,* or some similar response that lets you know they are not trying to defend themselves, but to help make it right.

Giving It Up and Gaining It All

We said earlier that humility could be seen as giving up the need to be greater than we are. We have looked at some ways in which that principle operates. It is giving up thinking that we know it all. Giving up thinking that we can do it all. Giving up thinking that we have to do it well all the time. Giving up thinking that we are better than others when they do not do it well. Giving up needing to be seen as right or good all the time, and giving up defensiveness. In all these cases, the way of the déjà vu person is basically to be real.

It is really true that we do not know it all, we do not have all the answers, we do not always get it right, we are just as imperfect as the next person, and we are not right or good all the time. No matter how great some person's particular talent or accomplishment, humility is always very available to him or her, and very evident to others. It does not take self-deprecation, such as *Oh, it was really nothing,* after some huge accomplishment. A simple *thank you* is a wonderful response. Although such a response seems to acknowledge one's own accomplishment, it does not show a lack of humility if in the rest of that person's life and interactions he or she is being real and honest. The accomplishments will not make such people proud or arrogant, because being real—acknowledging the reality of one's own human weaknesses and failures—will protect them from that. And it will endear others to them as well.

Déjà vu people accomplish great things. I have known some of them to be heads of large companies, professional star athletes, innovators, sacrificial humanitarians, television and movie celebrities, and leaders whose accomplishments in other fields are mind-blowing. But the difference between them and other so-called achievers is that they are successful in *all* of life. They are integrated, and unlike other people who accomplish things, they do not see success as *who* they are, and lord it over others; they see themselves as people just like everyone else, and they do all they can to love and serve those around them. As a result they succeed more. And unlike others who succeed, they do not blow it up in the end.

There are many people who achieve so-called "success." But if they are not humble, it gets tarnished by failed relationships, breaches in relationships that are never mended, unresolved battles with partners, moral collapse, and other blemishes that make their success of little benefit to them in the end. They destroy it.

Be a déjà vu person and learn the way of humility. When you do, not only will you succeed more, but you will also keep your success as well. Here are a few tips on the humble ways of déjà vu people:

- Say you are sorry to your children, spouse, coworkers, customers, and other people in your life when you fail them.

- Seek to understand situations and people before thinking you know the answer or the truth or what the reality actually is.

- Get rid of any and all defensiveness when it occurs in you. What you are defending—the need to be more than you are —is not worth keeping.

- Serve the people "under" you in whatever structures have placed you "over" them. In organizations where there are hierarchies, déjà vu people are as concerned with their relationship to the custodian as they are with their relationship to the CEO.

- The moment you think some task or position in life is beneath you, take a time out. Go spend some time with someone performing that task or in that position and you might meet a human being superior to yourself.

- Root out any attitude of entitlement that you may have. Embrace a spirit of gratitude for everything you have or any good treatment you get.

- When someone is hurt by you, listen. Try to understand what he or she is feeling and learn how you can make things better.

- Give up any investment in looking good, right, or any other posture that makes you different from the rest of humanity.

- Embrace your imperfections and the imperfections of others. Do not ever be surprised by them.

- Use failure as a teacher and a friend.

- *Be humble.*

11

PRINCIPLE 9:
UPSET THE RIGHT PEOPLE

*I cannot give you the formula for success, but I can give you the formula
for failure, which is try to please everybody.*

—HERBERT BAYARD SWOPE

M Y CLIENT, SIMON, was as nice a guy as you would ever
want to meet. He was always concerned about others,
often reached out to them, and was sensitive to their
feelings. As president of a sizable organization, he did many extra
things for the employees. He spent large amounts of money on
their personal growth and development, much more than the
industry average. I was impressed by his commitment to people
and their well-being. Because of his commitment to his employees,
I would never have guessed that he would do what he did—an act
which revealed his déjà vu nature.

Simon had been hired to turn the company around. It had
grown steadily for about twenty years when it hit a plateau. His
job was to return the organization to the growth rates that it had

experienced in its heyday. He was excited about the challenge, and he thought his experience matched it exactly.

But when he got into the midst of it all and began to study what was going on, he realized something. The solution to this company's stagnation was not going to be simply a matter of doing what they had been doing but doing it better, or even of adding radical innovations. He was going to have to restructure the entire operation from head to toe. That was the only way that the company would be able to adapt to the new market and meet its mission and purpose. As he expressed it, they would need to "turn it on its head and redo the whole thing."

That sounds like great fun for an energetic, creative person. And Simon was excited about it. But there was a catch. To do what he needed to do and what was right for the organization, the restructuring was going to be extremely painful in two significant ways. First, many employees would experience personal upheaval. They would lose their positions, get reassigned, be required to move, or even be laid off. Many people whom he cared for were going to be very upset and angry with him. Second, there were no short-term rewards to be had for Simon himself. The positive results of his actions would take a while to appear. Meanwhile he would look like the bad guy for at least a few years. People would think he had failed miserably.

Knowing Simon, I did not expect the second hurdle, the temptation to worry about what others thought of his performance, to be a big one for him. He was not the type to seek admiration and flattery from others. He did not do things for the sake of having a good image. But because he was such a people person, I did expect him to have a lot of conflict with the first hurdle. To cause so many people to be upset with him and put long-term relationships into serious conflict would be a very hard thing for him to do. As other-oriented as he was, I truly did not know if he could follow through, and I halfway expected a stall-out. What happened was exactly the opposite.

"Well, I announced the restructure," he told me. "It was the right thing to do, and the only way that we will be able to accomplish what I was hired for. But it has caused a storm of relational fallout. A lot of people are really mad at me now. I knew that was going to happen. So now I have to work things through with several people. It is going to be quite tough the next few months. I will spend hours and hours in one-on-one meetings with people I have known and worked with for years. It is not going to be fun."

I was stunned not only at his sense of resolve, but also with the fact that he had overcome the fear of other people's reactions. Then the déjà vu element hit me: in reality he had *not* overcome any fears of other people's reactions to his decision. Not at all. Why? *He never had that fear in the first place.* He accepted those reactions as a reality that would result from doing the right thing, but it never was a fear. It never entered his mind as a factor in the decision to do the right thing.

That was the characteristic I saw in Simon that made him a déjà vu person, one that I had seen consistently in truly successful people. While they are very loving and feel deeply the pain or distress that their decisions cause others. . . .

*Déjà vu people do not make decisions
based on the fear of other people's reactions.*

Successful people who practice this Principle Nine are sensitive to those reactions, but when weighing whether or not a given course is right, whether or not someone else is going to like it is not a factor that carries any weight. Concern, yes; but weight, no. Our déjà vu friends care about other people's feelings, but they do not base their decisions on them. They decide to do what is right first and deal with the fallout second.

This is true both in the world of work and the world of personal relationships. Successful people tend to be self-controlled, as we saw in chapter six. As we said then, when someone's locus of control is outside themselves, they never know where they are heading in life. Instead of their values, goals, and purposes determining their choices, other people's reactions do. As a result, they can end up all over the map, or as I thought my client Simon would do, they often stall out and find themselves unable to make a decision.

I love boating on the ocean. The boat's autopilot fascinates me to no end, and I love to follow the course corrections it makes as the boat travels. Here is how it works: the captain sets a compass heading for where he wants to go. He locks in that heading on the autopilot, and the boat takes off in that direction. So far, so good. But where it gets interesting is when the craft hits a large wave or a series of waves. The autopilot does not allow external actions to alter its course. It keeps its original decision in place, heads straight for the goal, and goes through the wave. There is a splash, lots of rocking and spray, and an *immediate* correction by the autopilot if the ship is knocked off course in any way. And when I say immediate, I mean immediate. The autopilot does not allow the ship to get swayed off its course even momentarily when it hits a bump in the water.

Most people don't operate this way. They know their ship's "heading," the direction in which they want to go, but they look out over the prow and see a wave—someone's adverse reaction to their decision. The wave looms larger and larger until it appears even bigger than their decision and the goals and values that drove that decision. So they change their course. They adjust their heading starboard to try to go around the wave. By then they have lost their heading. They avoided the crash into the wave and getting soaked by the spray, but they are now off course.

No, in reality that is not quite true. They are on course, but it is someone else's course, not theirs. *They have kept someone happy, but they have lost their own way.* As a result they will never get to where they wanted to go in the first place because there will always be another wave coming.

If they had not been afraid of getting a little wet or plowing through bumpy water, they would soon be well on their way. The bump would be behind them, and the sea would eventually smooth out and return to calm. If it did not, then there was a deeper problem in that sea of relationship to begin with, and no amount of pleasing or appeasing is likely to help.

So here we have the last of the Nine Things you must do to be a successful person. Let's look at some of the seas that have to be navigated in life with Principle Nine, and determine what waves they have that might tempt you to lose your way.

I Do Not Want to Hurt His Feelings

Sarah was at the end of her rope and had no more hope for her dating relationship with David. When they had begun dating, she thought he was the greatest. Attractive, in command of life, successful, intelligent, and charming were the words she used to describe him to her friends and family. She thought the search was over. Smitten, in a word.

But, as time went on, she had to add a few other words to the mix. Words like controlling and possessive. The enormous attention that she thought so incredible in the beginning soon became smothering. He could not stand for her to be away from him. If she had to be away for work or to take care of her own interests, he became angry or withdrawn. At first this behavior merely surprised her. It had never occurred to her that he had any insecurity at all, because he was so self-confident and assertive in the external world, and easily went after whatever he wanted. She had liked that about him. He seemed strong and aggressive.

After several months, however, she could not deny that David had some real insecurities for which he was not taking responsibility. She tried to get him to see that their relationship could not work if he could not allow her to have time for herself. She tried to talk him into getting counseling to help with his problem so things could work for them. But he would not. Finally, she decided to get the help herself, and that is when she came to me.

Sarah was in turmoil. She knew that she could not go on with David, for he was driving her crazy with his obsessive jealousy and control. I did not have to talk her into realizing that this was not a good foundation for a relationship, so I asked her why she had come. "How can I help?" I asked.

"I can't tell David that I want to end it," she said. "I just can't."

"Because of all the things you like about him? You find it hard to let go of all of his good parts?" I asked.

"No, not really. I mean, yes, but no," she said. "I will miss all the wonderful things about him. I hate letting go of that good stuff, but I don't fear it because I know that I will get over it."

"So, call him and end it," I said. "What is keeping you from doing that?"

"I just don't want to hurt his feelings," she said. "I feel so bad for him. I can't do it. I mean, I don't even have the heart to tell him I can't spend the weekend with him anymore. It hurts him too badly. But I know I don't want this long-term."

It took her several months to get out of the relationship with David. She would get all geared up, go for it, and guess what would happen: he would be devastated. He would talk to her about all the good that they had going and how he could not live without her. He would tell her that he loved her more than anyone ever would, and then ask how she could walk away from a love like that. And facing such a wave, she would agree and relent. She would cave in, have sex with him against her values, and swiftly, in one evening, find herself off course—right back in the relationship as deeply as ever, starting over again when what she desperately wanted was out. *His reaction would steer her off course.*

But slowly, through our work and the support of her friends, Sarah got back on course. She got out. What saddened me for her were three things, which became the focus of my work with her. First was the amount of precious time she had wasted with David in the prime of her dating life. She let more than a year pass after she really knew that it was not going to work. Secondly was the mental agony she went through in avoiding the inevitable. What should have been one evening of pain followed by an aftermath of temporary grief turned into months and months of breaking up, not breaking up, sort of breaking up, sort of getting back together, and all of the other ways to describe being entangled with, but not committed to, the wrong person. It was "bad pain," which basically means pain that serves no good purpose.

The third thing, though, and the big thing that we finally focused on, was this: in her over-dependence on other people's reactions to her decisions (in this case, being too concerned about David's hurt feelings), she had lost the ability to feel, find, define, clarify, know, and act upon what she wanted. She had lost herself in a bad way. Worried about his immature reactions, she had lost touch with the ability to know what she wanted because she was overly concerned with what David wanted. She had to learn to "upset the right people."

In the process of our work, she discovered that this tendency was affecting her negatively in many areas. She saw that in her work she had picked bad business partners and agreed to do projects that were not in her best interests. She had multiple ties and arrangements that she should not have gone into but could not see the dangers clearly enough because of her tendency to avoid disappointing people or making them angry. This tendency blinded her to other people's negative character issues, and she had made some bad choices. Because she was overly concerned about the reactions of others, she often did not see their character problems until later in the relationship.

At the same time, I had another client who was in a new relationship with a man. Same beginning—a guy who was attractive, winsome, energetic, accomplished, and all the rest. But after a few months when the possessiveness and control became apparent, she came in and said, "I had to end it with Reed. I just couldn't see living like that. I could not do anything for myself without it becoming an issue. That is not what I want in a relationship, so I broke it off. I will miss him though. He was pretty cool."

"How did he take it?" I asked.

"Not well," she said. "He was really upset and begged me to reconsider. He made all kinds of promises to change. He cried, and it was hard."

"What did you do?" I asked.

"I just told him I was sorry it had to be this way, but I did not want to be together anymore. Even though it was hurtful, it had to be. Then I left. I went over to Laura's for the night, because I was pretty upset afterward too. But I know it was right. If I hadn't done this, I would be dealing with the same issues forever. I don't want that."

That was the response of a déjà vu person. Hard to do, tough on both sides. She was considerate, but she would not be thrown off course. She knew the right thing to do, *and* she knew that his response was not going to be happy.

Those two things, as my friend Simon realized, are very different issues. And recognizing the difference is the déjà vu person's way to see this problem:

What you should do, and what someone's response
is going to be, are two very different issues.

And because they are different, déjà vu people do not mix them together. They do what they need to do, and then they figure out the best way to handle the situation with the other person's feelings. But they keep the two issues separated as two different problems.

Think of situations where being overly concerned about hurting someone's feelings can cause a person to stall out or drag a bad thing on too long:

- Firing a person

- Confronting a person

- Saying no to a request to do something that involves time, energy, money, or other resources

- Saying no to a request because it would violate one of your values

- Doing an intervention with someone because of her very destructive behavior

- Telling a person that he has overstayed his welcome

- Making someone aware of a flaw that she does not see in herself that is hurting her relationships with others

- Breaking up with a person you are dating or telling him that you are not interested

The Difference Between Hurt and Harm

One of the important distinctions that déjà vu people make in this situation is to understand the difference between hurting someone and harming him. Hurt is a normal part of life. Our feelings can be hurt when we get confronted, for example. We have to swallow our pride and look at something negative about ourselves, and that hurts. But it hurts like surgery hurts: it is good for us. It hurts, but it does not injure or harm us.

Getting rejected is like that. Hearing "no" hurts at times, too, especially if we really want something. Failing, or getting fired, stings. But those things do not harm us. They are a part of life, and we learn from them if we are looking at life correctly. Hearing hard truth can actually help us. As Solomon says, "Wounds from a friend can be trusted" (Proverbs 27:6). Hurt does not mean harm.

Harm is when we injure people by doing destructive things to them. We do not offensively inflict injury on another person when we make a decision to do something that pains him if it is done for a purpose, or for one's own well-being. Learn the old saying, *I am not doing this to you. I am doing it for me.*

That is not inflicting harm at all, even if the person on the receiving end acts as if it is.

AFTER ALL I'VE DONE FOR YOU . . .

Another barrier that many people feel when making decisions is guilt. When they choose to do something for themselves, or make any kind of decision based on their conviction that it is the right thing to do, they sometimes feel as if they have done something bad because of people's adverse reactions.

I had one déjà vu experience along these lines when a friend put his elderly mother in an assisted care facility. His family had been helping her in many ways as she got up in years. Although she was relatively healthy, the burden was getting to be too much for any of them. The situation had reached the point where their family life could not continue intact if she were not where she could get the kind of help they could not provide.

When my friend told his mother of their decision, she ranted at him with enough guilt messages to weigh down several families. "After all I've done for you," she began, and it went on from there. "Just send me away to die!" she said, even though she was perfectly capable of partaking in all sorts of activities at the facility if she chose. His response?

"Mom, I am sorry that it feels to you like we don't care. Certainly we do. And we are going to visit often. But we just cannot take care of you at home anymore. This is the best decision. Now, you have a choice. You can be angry about it and refuse to enjoy this wonderful facility and all the great people here. You can sulk and miss out on its benefits. Or you can try to enjoy it, take part, meet the people and have a good life with them and with us. It is up to you. I will help you, but you are going to have to choose to make this work for you," he said.

He hit the wave in a turbulent sea. She did not like it. Spraying guilt upon guilt, she tried to steer the ship onto an alternate course. But he was fixed on a heading and did not allow the guilt message to get him off the course he had set as best for his own family and her as well.

"Do Not Rescue an Angry Man"

I was on a financial radio show recently taking calls about setting boundaries in families with financial issues. A woman called about her forty-year-old sister to whom she and her husband had been giving money for several years. It seemed that the sister had a lot of problems and "needed their help," as she put it. But the caller was beginning to wonder if helping was really helping. In other words, in spite of all the "help" they had given her sister, she was not getting any more self-sufficient.

"Does she work?" I asked.

"No, she lives off my father's Social Security," she said. "But that, along with some other family money, does not seem to be enough. Or, more accurately, she always seems to overspend what she has coming in. So we always help her out in the crunch. My husband and I are getting tired of it."

"Has she had mental illness or some disability that keeps her from working?" I asked.

"Well, she has seen a lot of counselors, but she always quits before they do her any good. She is on some kind of medication, but there is nothing really wrong with her that would keep her from working. She gets a lot of jobs but then quits after a few days when they want her to do something she doesn't want to do."

"If there is no real reason that she cannot work," I said, "and no real danger from illness or disability, then why don't you set up some requirements for her to meet if you are going to give her money? For example, you could insist that she stay in counseling and do some work or you are not going to support her. Anytime we support someone, there should be structure to it with clear expectations understood by the recipient and enforced by the giver. Why don't you do that?"

"Well, our experience is that whenever we withhold help from her, she gets really mad," she explained. "She blows up and blames us for her problems. We don't want to make that happen again."

"Let me tell you something," I said. *"There is a direct correlation with people who are out of control in their lives and their hatred of the word* no. You usually do not see responsible people get angry and go on the attack just because they do not get what they want. But often you do see irresponsible people getting mad when they hear no. Just like toddlers who do not get what they want, they throw a tantrum. And if you give in to it, you will find out how true the words of Solomon are. He said, 'Do not rescue an angry man, lest you have to do it again tomorrow' (Proverbs 19:19, my paraphrase). In other words, if you give in once to her anger, get ready to do it again the next time you say no."

That is the thing to remember about trying to appease controlling and angry people. If you let their anger decide your course of action for you—whether to give or not to give—then you have just trained them in how to get what they want out of you. You have set yourself up for the same experience again.

In addition, do you really want to give to someone who is only going to hate you if you do not? What kind of a relationship is that? What kind of love is that? True love would accept your choice and respect your having to say no.

If you are resetting your course based on the fact that someone might get angry with you, you have chosen a flimsy foundation upon which to make a decision. You have lost control of yourself, and that is not what successful people do. They are not held hostage by anger.

As a footnote to this discussion, I will tell you that I am seeing a disturbing trend. I have no empirical evidence to back this up—only anecdotal. As I make live media appearances and do seminars around the country, I am getting an increase of questions from parents of adults who have been supporting their adult children well into their twenties, thirties, and even forties, but with a particular twist. When the parents cut off these "children" and stop paying for their lives of nonwork, the children are getting angry with the parents for not supporting them as adults! I actually get that situation fairly regularly, and I cannot remember that being the case ten or fifteen years ago.

Is there something different about this generation? Did some of the baby-boomer parents who rebelled against authority in the sixties not set the needed limits and impart discipline to their kids when they were growing up, causing those kids to enter adulthood not knowing what "no" means? Or does it just mean that the baby boomers are the first generation that has had the resources to continue to support their adult children? Who knows? Whatever the reason, if you have adult children, do not allow their temper tantrums to control your life. Déjà vu people would never do that!

A related scenario I often encounter on radio or at seminars involves a person whose spouse needs serious confrontation and limits, but the fear of an angry response to confrontation keeps the bad situation stuck in place. For example, a woman called recently and described a husband with a drinking problem who was ignoring his responsibilities as a father and husband. Her way of dealing with him was to alternate between appeasement and whiny nagging that was disguised as making requests of him to meet his obligations.

I suggested that if he were not responding to those appeals—alcoholics typically do not—then a more direct confrontation would have a better chance, especially if it required him to seek treatment or face consequences. Her response revealed the dynamic that was the glue for this problem's ability to stick around for so many years: "I can't do that! He would get angry!"

There it is in a nutshell. She could not do the right thing because of his reaction. "Of course he will get angry," I said. "That's what alcoholics do when they are confronted. That is their job! But your job is to have the proper resources there with support, or even professionals, to not let his anger dictate what is going to happen."

I continued, "Do not give him control of what you do, or what the interventionist says, or what choices are given to him just because he gets angry. Who cares if he is angry? That is part of his sickness, and we expect it. Just because the patient screams does not keep the doctor from administering the shot. As long as you stay the course, he is only in control of himself and whether or not he gets with the program. His anger cannot dictate what his options are going to be. Even if he is angry, the rest of you can still tell him the way it is going to be, what he has to do to keep living in your home, or whatever consequences you and your support team have decided upon."

It was as if aliens had landed in her yard. She was stunned that she or anyone could continue to follow a plan or maintain choices in the face of his anger. For the first time, a little realization dawned on her that his anger was not the compass to which everyone else set their heading.

LOSS OF APPROVAL OR LOVE

Sometimes those who need to confront are afraid of not only a negative response such as anger or guilt, but the loss of something positive that they value too highly to risk. Earlier in this chapter when we looked at Simon's choices, we noted that he faced two possible scenarios, each of which were going to prove difficult. One was that people would be upset, and the other was the loss of Simon's short-term rewards, such as people thinking he was doing a great job and looking up to him as a successful leader. For Simon, being a déjà vu person, this temporary loss of a positive image was not a problem. But for some people, the fear of losing others' approval or love is a big value, bigger even than doing what they need to do to solve a problem.

I had a client who was a very successful pastor. His work has touched the lives of millions of people. He is well respected by all who know him and his work, and his family is immensely proud of him. But it was not always so.

His father owned a successful family business and was well known in his industry, amassing a lot of power, wealth, and influence. And with the business being in the family and so successful, it was assumed that the only son would follow in Dad's footsteps and succeed him as president of the company.

But, in college, my client received a different call. He dived into his faith wholeheartedly as a sophomore, and by his senior year he knew that the ministry was his future. He was excited, but he knew his family would not be. Who would take over the business? What would his father say? While he did not know the answer to the first question, he had a pretty good idea about the second. Because his father was a person who was used to getting his own way, my friend would most likely lose his father's approval. And that is exactly what happened.

The onslaught was furious. His father, though a professing Christian, had little respect for people outside of the business world. He thought that if you were a "real man," as he put it, you would do a "real man's job." Seeing the ministry as a softer vocation than industry, he questioned his son's manhood, his devotion to the family, his strength, and other character traits. It was an awful time for my client.

But, through his déjà vu character and the strength that God gave him, he did not change his course. He was saddened by the loss of his father's approval, but like other déjà vu people *he saw that as a separate issue from the decision itself.* He had to make a decision about his life, and also he had to deal with his relationship with his father. He did the right thing and encountered the waves with his father, thus demonstrating the strong character his father was saying he did not have, an interesting paradox in itself. If he were weak, like his father said he was, then he would have caved in and done what his father said a strong person would do. The reality was exactly the opposite. His strength was what enabled him to do what his father perceived as less manly.

Years have passed now, and the two men are reconciled. It took a while, and in the beginning of his ministry his father did not show his son a lot of respect. As the son's ministry has grown, his father is now beaming proud of him, as well he should be. But if my client had given in to the loss of his father's approval, there would be no one for the father to be proud of, only a "successful" puppet.

That is never the way of déjà vu people. They go against the odds if the odds are against what is right. They are willing to be the odd one, risking loss of approval in order to do the right thing. They understand that the approval of others does not go very far in making one truly fulfilled. It may be nice for a moment, but getting up every day and doing what you believe in is much more lasting.

Learning to Upset the Right People

In one of my seminars a woman once asked, "Dr. Cloud, how do you deal with controlling people?"

"You convert them," I said.

"What?" she replied, assuming that I meant a religious conversion. "To what?"

"Convert them from being controlling to being frustrated," I answered. "The only way people can be controlling is for you to make them that way by doing what they want. Here is what happens: They get angry, or use guilt, or get pushy, and you give in. Then you come here and describe them as controlling. In reality, if you did not do what they wanted, you could not describe them as controlling, could you? If you say no to them and do not do what they are demanding, then they have no control of you. So you cannot say they are controlling at all; they are in control of nothing. They are just frustrated as they try to get control of you. You have converted them from being controlling to being frustrated simply by not giving in to their demands. It is that simple."

I went on to give examples of ways to maintain the relationship by empathizing. You can say something like this:

"I am so sorry it is frustrating to you when I say no. I can see it is hard for you to accept."

"I am sorry that it feels to you like I don't care. That must be difficult. But I do hope you can see that I do care."

"I am sorry it is so frustrating to you that I am making this choice. I hope you can accept that I still care about you even though I have decided to do this for me."

That is what déjà vu people do when others give problematic reactions to their choices. They do not return the anger, as we saw in chapter nine. They give better than that. They give love, care, sensitivity, and empathy. They do not become reactive; they listen and care. But they do not give in. Instead they follow a parallel track of giving love and keeping their stand intact. "I love you, Dad. And I am going to be a pastor. I know that must be very disappointing to you. I am sorry it is so hard."

STRATEGY IS NOT BAD

Déjà vu people who do not base their decisions on the reactions of others are not foolish. If they expect the person being confronted to go ballistic, or retaliate, or do something destructive, wise people take that into account. For example, in the case of the woman calling about her alcoholic husband, I suggested that she confront him with professional alcohol counselors present, as well as other supportive people. There are many situations that require strategy and discretion. If the problem person is out of control and dangerous, the wise strategy may be not to confront, but to keep quiet and go to a shelter.

At other times and in other situations, such as negotiations, it is smart to foresee how a person is going to react and plan a strategy as to how you are going to manage that reaction or deal with it. Taking such extreme reactions into account and strategizing to deal with them has nothing to do with fearing them. Dealing with such reactions wisely is not the same as letting fear of them control your decisions. The problem scenarios are those in which feared reactions either dictate the course you take or allow the reactive person to gain control of you. It is fine to use a smart strategy to deal with them and avoid unnecessary conflict and chaos. Life is too short to put up with that stuff. You just cannot let reactive people steer your life course.

SET YOUR HEADING

To be a successful déjà vu person, you may not keep everyone around you happy. In fact, if you are successful in life, you are guaranteed not to! Jesus said it best: "Woe to you when all men speak well of you" (Luke 6:26). When *all* people speak well of you, it means that you are duplicitous and a people-pleaser. You cannot speak the truth, live out good values, and choose your own direction without disappointing some people.

The key is not to count your critics, but instead to weigh them. Do not try to avoid upsetting people; *just make sure that you are upsetting the right ones.* If the kind, loving, responsible, and honest people are upset with you, then you had better look at the choices you are making. But if the controlling, hot and cold, irresponsible, or manipulative people are upset with you, then take courage! That might be a sign that you are doing the right thing and becoming a déjà vu person!

12

BECOMING A
DÉJÀ VU PERSON

I WILL NEVER FORGET THAT DAY. I was in college, and I was wondering how people became successful. How did they make relationships work? How did they accomplish their goals and build a life that was satisfying and fulfilling? As I sat in my room on that particular day, everything looked pretty dark to me.

I had gone to school with high hopes for a sports career, but that dream was chronically hampered and finally ended by a tendon injury. After the injury I had tried to find an alternative, something I wanted to do and could really sink my teeth into. But I was having no luck. It seemed that none of the courses I took and none of the areas I looked into really grabbed me. And looming even larger than that, I wondered how success would come to me even if I did find the field that I liked. There seemed to be many steps involved and many abilities present in those who had "made it" that were foreign to me—at least I felt that they were foreign to me.

To make my mood even darker, I had just gone through a

breakup with a girlfriend with whom I was quite serious. It made me wonder how a good relationship is found or made to last. At that moment, success seemed pretty unattainable to me, both in love and life. Then something happened.

For some reason, I had the thought that I should look in the Bible. That was not something I had done much since arriving at college. I was too deeply involved in other things to think about my spiritual life. But on that day I was at the bottom, so when the thought came I was more open to spiritual direction than usual. When I opened the book, I came upon a verse that seemed to jump out at me. It was from a section where Jesus was saying that worrying about life (exactly what I was doing at that moment) does not get us very far in accomplishing the life that we desire. Instead, he pointed to a different path:

> *So do not worry, saying, "What shall we eat?" or "What shall we drink?" or "What shall we wear?" For the pagans run after all these things, and your heavenly Father knows that you need them. But seek first his kingdom and his righteousness, and all these things will be given to you as well. Therefore do not worry about tomorrow, for tomorrow will worry about itself. Each day has enough trouble of its own.*
> —MATTHEW 6:31–34

On that particular day, I did not know what all Jesus meant in those verses, but I did know that the way I was going about things was not working. So I decided to try it his way. I told him that I wanted help, that my life was not working, and that I needed him to show me the way to make it all come together. I guess you could call it that "leap of faith" that people talk about. I did not know what else to do, nor did I know what would happen next. In my naiveté, I was hoping he might just come down and "make it all better." And, in a real sense, that is exactly what he did. But, *how he did it* was far from what I expected. There were no lightening bolts, no instructions written across the sky.

What he did was this: immediately he put people around me who knew the path I was seeking and who helped me to go step by step onto that path. Some of them you have met in this book, but there were others as well. In all of that I discovered a great truth, and all the déjà vu people I have ever known have told me it has been true for them as well: *God puts people in our lives who show us the way.*

These God-sent people are models for us. They show us how to grow and what steps to take. They push us, correct us, support us, and discipline us. And as they do all of that, we have to do some things as well: we have to become what God and others are showing us we need to be. We have to be engaged in the process and take the steps to become who he created us to be. That is the meaning of the part of the verse about seeking his kingdom and his righteousness. It means we need to learn his ways and become a person who learns more and more how to do it "right."

On that day I discovered four things that changed my life. They were the same four things that I have heard other people affirm countless times:

1. God is there to help us if we ask him.

2. He not only helps us directly, he gives us others to help as well.

3. There are truths and principles, ways as we have called them, that are the ways he designed life to work.

4. As we practice those ways, good things are given.

I want to encourage you to employ these same four steps as you put the Nine Things into practice. I believe that God will help you. He will also give you people to help you, and he will reveal the truths you need to learn to put into practice. Your job is to actively embrace these four steps as you learn the Nine Things.

It is an exciting journey, and one that can yield incredible results in all areas of your life. But you will face challenges along the way. In that light, I want to end the book with a few helpful hints that will help make the journey go more smoothly and be more fruitful. I have seen these hints proven effective countless times. In fact, often when I have seen people fail to accomplish growth, it has been due to the absence of some of the principles I will pass on to you in these hints.

Some of the items that follow may seem familiar to you because we have hit on them briefly in previous chapters. But I list them here as stepping stones on the path of applying the Nine Things.

Twelve Steps to Applying the Nine Things

1. Do Not Go It Alone

Over and over in this book, you have seen examples of people "doing it well." Whether building a business, a career, or a relationship, they seemed to do the right thing at the right time. But none of them ever got there on his or her own. They all had help becoming the person that did it well.

Some got training and support from their parents and families. Others got it from a support group or a therapist. Still others learned from mentors and friends. But, as the Bible tells us, none of us has anything that was not given to us in some form or fashion. While some people may claim to be "self-made," someone taught them how to read or put them in time-out until they learned the self-discipline needed to accomplish their feats. We all get it from somewhere.

So, as you look at the Nine Things and desire to practice them, look to wise, loving people to help you. Find a support group, a counselor, or a coach. There is no magic formula that tells you where help has to come from. But there is a formula that says if you do not have help, you are not going to get as far. Listen again to Solomon:

> *Two are better than one,*
> *because they have a good return for their work:*
> *If one falls down,*
> *his friend can help him up.*
> *But pity the man who falls*
> *and has no one to help him up!*
> *Also, if two lie down together, they will keep warm.*
> *But how can one keep warm alone?*
> *Though one may be overpowered,*
> *two can defend themselves.*
> *A cord of three strands is not quickly broken.*
>
> —ECCLESIASTES 4:9–12

So, as the wisest man wrote, and countless déjà vu people have proven, "Do not go it alone."

2. Receive Wisdom

Not only do we need support and strength from others, we must recognize that we have a lot to learn as well. Whether it is in building relationships, a career, or a dream, there are things we need to know to get there. Seek that wisdom from those who know and have already done what you are seeking to do.

Read, study, go to seminars, take classes, research, hang around the ones who do it well. In short, take in all the information you can find that relates to what you want to do. You will get back much more than you invest. Solomon says it this way: "Wisdom is supreme; therefore get wisdom. Though it cost all you have, get understanding" (Proverbs 4:7).

3. Receive Feedback and Correction

As we saw in chapter ten on Principle Eight ("Be Humble"), wise people receive feedback well. I repeat it here as part of the process of becoming a déjà vu person. Remember, if you had it all together, you would already be there. So, just get comfortable with the fact that there are things about yourself and your ways that need correction. If you do that, you will be open to the answers when they come, and with each correction you will be one step closer to your goal.

4. Find Models

We cannot easily do what we have never seen done. My déjà vu friends were great models to watch, and I learned tremendously from seeing how they did love and life. It helped me immeasurably to see them in action, and all of them would tell you that they had models as well.

Your models can be people you know well, like mentors, friends, or coaches. Or they can be people you "watch" through studying their stories and seeing how they behave. It is the watching and imitating that takes this step a little further than step number one ("Do Not Go It Alone"). While that point refers to active support, coaching, encouragement, and correction that others provide, this one is specific to watching what the successful ones do. It is about seeing it done before you can do it.

5. Review Your Patterns

In the past when you have set out on a new course and failed, what happened? When you failed, did you notice that you tended to fail in the same way each time, no matter what the goal? In other words, is there a pattern to the way you fail? For example, have you begun well and then dropped out? Have you folded when you hit an obstacle? Have you found yourself distracted from your set path by a new goal? When you've run into criticism, have you given up?

Look back at what has stopped you before and then apply the quarantine principle explained in step 10 that follows. Do not allow past patterns of failing to repeat themselves. To keep past failures from recurring, you must know the triggers that cause them to repeat. Arming yourself against the patterns and the triggers that set them off will give you protection when they come around again.

6. Deal with Impediments

There are times when our hurt, pain, or weakness gets in the way of our ability to practice the Nine Things. For example, you may be so afraid of rejection that Principle Two ("Pull the Tooth") in the form of a direct confrontation is hard for you. You have an impediment of fear. Not only do you need to grow in your confrontation skills, but you also must deal with the fear that is holding you back.

If you have clinical issues such as depression or anxiety, get help. By resolving those fears and hurts, you will find more freedom to practice and execute the Nine Things. See a good psychologist or counselor, join a group or a program. That is what wise déjà vu people do when something holds them back.

7. Add Structure

Sometimes outside structure is needed to accomplish things for which you lack the discipline to accomplish alone. *Play the movie* as you learned to do in chapter five, and you can see how things will look one year from now if you make yet one more effort to reach your goal without discipline. If you have not been able to reach it outside a structured program, then make the decision to find a structured program and join it.

As we said earlier, there is really no such thing as self-help, and this is especially true when it comes to finding discipline. But there are sources where we can find the discipline and structure that we do not possess. That is why addicts go to structured AA programs or treatment facilities. That is why people join Weight Watchers or some other good program for losing weight. That is why those who do not own an ant farm join groups designed to help them finish their dissertations. That is why those who cannot work out on their own join a class at a health club or hire a personal trainer. Remember the axiom: If you have not had the discipline to do it on your own, you will not gain it by gritting your teeth and making one more try alone. Add the structure from the outside.

8. Practice, Practice, Practice, and Fail

Growth is a process. Give up your demand to have it all together right now. Whatever you choose to accomplish, you will get it wrong more than once as you move toward your goal. Failure is part of the process, and no one who ever got there did it without failing. No one. You gain your place on that long list of winners by becoming a good loser. Get used to it. A winner is someone who steps out, fails, regroups, and instead of beating himself up, learns from the mistake and tries again.

That is what a winner is—a good loser. Because good losers—those who learn and try again—become winners in the end. The losers in life either do not lose well, or they avoid losing altogether by not trying in the first place. They avoid losing, and thus they avoid winning as well.

9. Change Your Beliefs

As you embark on this path of growth, you will find that forward movement exposes old belief systems that will try to deter you from your goal. *I will never succeed. Success is for other people, not me. This will never work. They will think I'm stupid.* There is no short-age of old beliefs that can hold you back.

But remember this: no matter how pervasive those beliefs are in your head, they have nothing to do with future reality. They are only old beliefs or voices from times gone by.

How do you banish these false beliefs? First, you identify them by listening to how you talk to yourself. Keep a journal of those negative thoughts. Write down where they come from—what experience in your life planted such pessimism? Then change each negative belief into a positive one that reflects the way you want to believe and can be translated into reality. Learn to talk back to those debilitating beliefs as you hear them come up in your head. Research has shown over and over that as people monitor and challenge those belief systems, their lives change. And, as they fail to do that, they often remain stuck.

10. Quarantine Your Weaknesses

As we have seen, the déjà vu person is aware of his weaknesses, works on them, and tries to change them. But, he also respects them. If you have a particular weakness or pattern that has derailed you in the past, make sure that you protect yourself from it.

We saw this principle in chapter five on Principle Three, but we bring it up here as a reminder as you engage in the process. Your weaknesses do not just go away because you set a new goal. Some of your weaknesses are activated by "triggers." You must learn your triggers and make sure you are protected from them. Otherwise they will lead you into the same failure as before.

11. Put Your Vision and Goals on Paper

If you have no plan or goals to get you somewhere, you will end up nowhere. But if you have written out your visions and goals, you are more likely to reach them. Write down the big vision and plan out small but achievable steps that will get you there. Put dates to each step. Have your accountability partners hold you to those dates. Review your plan often.

Remember from chapter seven ("Act Like an Ant"): it was not enough for me to have as a goal *write a dissertation*. I needed several small steps with their own deadlines, such as "Have lunch with the advisor and land on a topic by March 1." Structured goals tend to turn themselves into reality when they are written down and accounted for.

12. *Pray, Pray, Pray*

Jesus said that the one who asks, seeks, and knocks will receive. Prayer is simple conversation with God, the Source of all that we need. He knows the answers to our dilemmas; he knows where the resources we need are to be found, and he knows the ways in which we need to change. If you ask him, he will answer. This is no magic formula or quick fix. Often we do not even see his answers except in retrospect. We find out later that a firm "no" was the best thing he could have given us when we wanted something that was not best for us. Whether we see him answer directly and quickly or find it out later, he always answers. And his answers are always for our good, even when they do not seem that way at the moment.

Each step of every day, practice what I refer to as "parallel consciousness." While you are performing any task, be asking him all the while for help. You will be surprised at how present he becomes in every area of your life.

If you have never met Jesus and desire a relationship with him, he told us how to do it and issued each person a challenge to find out whether he is real or not. He said, "Here I am! I stand at the door and knock. If anyone hears my voice and opens the door, I will come in and eat with him, and he with me" (Revelation 3:20).

He claimed to be God and he claims to be alive today. Test this claim for yourself. Ask him sincerely if he really is alive and really is there. If you do this, he will show up. You will never be alone again if you put your trust in him as Messiah and Lord. Then, ask him to relieve you of your worries and help you along the path toward what you are trying to accomplish. He promises to be a Shepherd to you for the rest of your life.

THE NINE THINGS ARE FOR EVERYONE

I want to leave you with a reminder of one thing I said in the beginning. It is something that watching my déjà vu friends taught me: *the "ways" we have discussed in these chapters are available to us all.* Do not see success in love or life as a goal that you cannot attain or a prize only for special or lucky people. That is not true. Success is never embodied in a person, but in the ways of wisdom that transcend any one individual. What déjà vu individuals do is find those ways and practice them. They are not special people, but ordinary people who are connected to these special ways.

My hope is that you might realize that these ways are available to you as well. And that you will embark on a path of putting them to practice in your own life and become a déjà vu person. If you stay on that path, I look forward to the time when I can meet you and see you do or say something that seems small and insignificant to you but seems vaguely familiar to me . . . déjà vu!